ALSO BY ROBERT McDOWELL

Poetry

Quiet Money
The Diviners
On Foot, In Flames

Translation

How I Came to Know Fish
by Ota Pavel (Jindriska Badal cotranslator)

Criticism

Poetry After Modernism (editor)
Sound and Form in Modern Poetry (coauthor)
The Reaper Essays (coauthor)
*Cowboy Poetry Matters: From Abilene to the Mainstream:
Contemporary Cowboy Writing* (editor)
One-Man Boat: Collected Writing of George Hitchcock
(coeditor)

Reading, Writing, and
Using Poetry in Your
Daily Rituals,
Aspirations,
and Intentions

Poetry as Spiritual Practice

Robert McDowell

FREE PRESS

New York London Toronto Sydney

*f*P

FREE PRESS

A Division of Simon & Schuster, Inc.
1230 Avenue of the Americas
New York, NY 10020

First Free Press hardcover edition July 2008

FREE PRESS and colophon are trademarks of
Simon & Schuster, Inc.

For information about special discounts for bulk pur-
chases, please contact Simon & Schuster Special Sales at
1-800-456-6798 or business@simonandschuster.com

Book design by Ellen R. Sasahara

Manufactured in the United States of America

1   3   5   7   9   10   8   6   4   2

Library of Congress Cataloging-in-Publication Data
McDowell, Robert.
Poetry as spiritual practice / Robert McDowell
p. cm.
1. Religion and poetry. 2. Poetry. I. Title.
PN1077.M35 2008
808.1—dc22   2007050310

ISBN-13: 978-1-4165-6650-2
ISBN-10:   1-4165-6650-3

*For Dana Gerhardt, who woke me up
and walks with me on the path,
all my love and adoration.*

Love follows knowledge.

—THOMAS AQUINAS

Contents

FOUR

Three Genres for Practice   213

Poetry as Spiritual Practice

Introduction

You ask what it's like when I meditate.
Watching birds.

Why should I read *Poetry as Spiritual Practice*?
   Poetry—writing it, reading it, and sharing it—provides insight into all mysteries and pursuits. Poetry does not exist for a select few; it is not a secret code that is almost impossible to crack. We know that we can learn the law, medicine, music, languages, a trade; we can learn to split the atom, pilot a plane, ride a horse, hit a baseball, make magic on a skateboard, climb mountains, drive an eighteen-wheeler, operate a fleshing machine, repair plumbing.

In the same way, we can learn to write and read poetry—*you* can learn to read and write poetry—and we can learn to share poetry, its beauty, wisdom, and lessons, with others. In doing so, we enhance our abilities in our chosen life paths as well as our work. Most important, we wake up to poetry's essence, its spirit. It is as if a long-settled cloud in our mind suddenly dissipates and we are divine once again. We see the poetry in life

1

around us and we can incorporate it into our daily lives and our spiritual practices.

All human beings—Christian, Jew, Hindu, Muslim, Buddhist, Taoist, animist, or atheist—seek spirituality in their daily lives whether they know it or not. We seek truths greater than ourselves, our individual beings. We desire peace and understanding. Throughout time, poetry has rewarded those who discovered its unique power. Through poetry, we gain greater self-understanding as well as insight into others in our world and into our world itself. It helps us discover the world anew, as if for the very first time—again and again—as each one of us must. This book will guide you on your spiritual quest, revealing poetry for inner peace and inspiration created by some of the most renowned spiritual leaders of every age. And it will explain how you, too, can enrich your spiritual practice, give deeper meaning to your life, and achieve your goals.

But just what *is* poetry as spiritual practice?

It is reading poems, writing your own poems, and making them part of your daily rituals, aspirations, and intentions. By assuming certain postures, participating in call-and-response, meditating and reciting poems, chants, hymns, prayers, mantras, songs, and scripture, you make of yourself a tuning fork ready for the thwack of the Divine.

The Trappist monk André Louf describes this process as a kind of fermentation, a ripening and welling up of the Word " . . . that has become wholly our own . . . inscribed deep in our body and psyche. . . . It bubbles up, it flows, it runs like living water." No matter what you practice, the goal is Reunion with the Word and the shedding of ego, until "it is no longer we who pray, but the prayer prays itself in us."

Poetry is this reverberating note, this pure sound and shape of your spirit as it makes sense to you at last. Through the almost musical vibration, you move from individual soul out into the Oversoul.

We knew that sound and its vibration as children, and even before that. In the womb, through mother's breath and heartbeat, our first meters, echoes, rhymes, and rhythms were embedded in our nervous systems. As infants and toddlers, our earliest sleep songs, comfort songs, and memorization work entered us in the forms of chants and metered lines that were built to be remembered. These lessons continued as we began school and received our first religious instruction.

But as schools and religions grew over the last fifty years into formidable corporate identities, they have increasingly turned from the magic of poetry to the more manageable, quantitative pleasures of test scores and egoistic Us versus Them dogma. Since the 1970s, this is the byway on which so many of us have been stuck. Without consciously realizing it, we accepted that, as religions became big businesses, they expelled poetry from the canon in much the same way that Plato banished it from his ideal Republic. Though Plato himself has been marginalized in much of the current curricula, his arguments still influence our thought whether we know it or not. Plato acknowledged Homer's greatness, which educated ancient Greece through the *Iliad* and the *Odyssey*, but saw grave threats to society's stability in the works of Homer's followers and interpreters, arguing for philosophy as a more desirable, steady discipline, and attacking poetry's unpredictability and influence on emotion. Philosophy, Plato argued, was just the thing to reign in popular culture and correct society's errant course.

Today administrators in education and religion have largely replaced philosophers, poets, and teachers as shapers of policy in their fields. They've established educational and religious regimens that originate in statistics and profits. They distrust the imagination and spiritual inquiry.

In our schools, grades K through 12, students are not so much educated as trained to perform well on standardized tests. They aren't taught to think for themselves, question, or be curious. They're encouraged to accept what they're told without hesitation. Could this have something to do with the fact that more than 50 percent of eligible young people in the United States do not bother to vote, or with America's free fall among other nations when comparing what students know in language arts, math, and science?

Just as our schools have choked off the poetry in us by teaching it less and less, our big-business religions have also estranged us from imagination and rigorous spiritual inquiry. When religions grow into organizations, their individual members diminish, becoming pawns in political campaigns or cash cows in fundraisers. Internal dissent and debate are discouraged. Some who attend services do so more out of habit than devotion. Their prayers do not emanate from the heart. Although the words are still poetry, their meaning and passion are obscured.

As a result, we develop a gnawing hunger. We know that we want and need more from spiritual practice. We want to work harder, be bolder, and connect with divine words that still resonate inside. We yearn for the return of poetry to spiritual practice. To rediscover its power, we must integrate reading and writing poetry into our individual lives.

People throughout history have known this inner bliss,

this awareness that the Divine's voice is inside you. San Juan de la Cruz (later known as Saint John of the Cross) discovered poetry as spiritual practice in prison (*this highest knowledge lies / in the loftiest sense / of the essence of God*), where his suffering was transformed by a series of divine consolations that inspired him to write. Borrowing poetic images from the *Song of Songs*, this sixteenth-century monk broke through personal spiritual despair to enlightenment, composing some of the most venerable poems in Spanish literature. His poems have inspired millions, including his friend and fellow reformer, Saint Teresa of Ávila, whose ecstatic poetry expresses the passion and surrender of one who celebrates a union with God, who she envisions as diving into us wholly and completely, becoming an ever-present part of us.

The twelfth-century religious teacher, Hildegard of Bingen, was also a visionary who perceived that the Word and God are inseparable (*No creature has meaning / without the Word of God*). She wrote poetry and hymns that celebrated her conversations and relationship with God. In her early years, Hildegard doubted the visions that inspired her writing and teaching, but in time grew to trust the communiqués from the Divine, her own inner poetry.

Of course, poetry as spiritual practice is not limited to Catholic saints or to Catholics. In India centuries ago, Mirabai faced an arranged marriage and a life of domestic servitude, in the custom of her culture. Mirabai rebelled and, as leader of a band of sympathetic women, she wandered the country creating and reciting poems praising Krishna, her God and spiritual husband. They express, as Sri Chinmoy so beautifully observes, "her inspiration, aspiration and sleepless self-giving." Mirabai's poem-songs still enrich spiritual practice and energize popular culture. She is revered as one of India's most beloved saints. One of the country's most prolific film companies, Mirabai Productions, is named after her.

The Sufi poets Hafiz and Rumi wrote hundreds of religious poems ecstatically celebrating the relationship between God and humanity. Poems by contemporary spiritual mentors including the Dalai Lama, Adyashanti, Deepak Chopra, Sri Chinmoy, and Thich Nhat Hanh, among others, also explore the spiritual union between people and a higher power.

Poetry as spiritual practice is for everyone, no matter your religion or spiritual background. As spiritual poet Robert Bly described our time: " . . . the impulse for reverence endures . . . . Reclaiming the sacred in our lives naturally brings us close once more to the wellsprings of poetry." *Poetry as Spiritual Practice* can lead you to those wellsprings, where you'll remember, or discover for the first time, that poetry is the language of devotion.

Just as any practice done well requires focus, poetry as spiritual practice requires unwavering presence in the moment. This can be a challenge, even for the most thoughtful, awake person. Our brains are busy, often cluttered, like a closet in which we store things and never get around to cleaning out. They're forever filling, processing, and mixing, even as we sleep. Spiritual practice helps us clear space and create order out of confusion, but spiritual *poetry* practice makes possible even greater discernment, clarity, and attention to detail.

Robert Frost said that poetry doesn't so much tell us anything new, but reminds us of things that we need to know but forgot. You may already be using poetry as spiritual practice without knowing it, in which case this book will help you remember, identify, and deepen your experience.

A man I know is devoted to his spiritual life and recites dozens of mantras and prayers daily. He doubted that poetry would help him, but when he described his spiritual practice for me, he said that it began and ended with the Lord's Prayer, and he recited mantras and meditated for twenty minutes on peace, compassion, love, patience, or whatever area concerned him most on a given day. He added that, on occasion, when he was stressed out at work or had had an argument at home, he benefited by reciting this prayer:

Lord, make me a channel of thy peace,
That where there is hatred, I may bring love;
That where there is wrong, I may bring the spirit of
    forgiveness;
That where there is discord, I may bring harmony;
That where there is error, I may bring truth;
That where there is doubt, I may bring faith;
That where there is despair, I may bring hope;
That where there are shadows, I may bring light;
That where there is sadness, I may bring joy.
Lord, grant that I may seek rather to comfort than to be
    comforted;
To understand, than to be understood;
To love, than to be loved.
For it is by self-forgetting that one finds.
It is by forgiving that one is forgiven.
It is by dying that one awakens to Eternal Life.

A priest in Geneva had taught it to him on a rainy, shut-in day many years ago. He didn't know why he loved it so much; the words always made him feel as if his spine were tingling.

He'd smile, feeling more centered, or closer to God. He was surprised when I told him that *The Prayer of Saint Francis* is in fact a poem, that its metrical regularity and repetitive punctuation (those semicolons!) have a lot to do with the pleasing physical sensations he experiences.

If you're after proof of the benefits of poetry as spiritual practice on a massive scale, I can think of no better example than *The Serenity Prayer*:

> God give us grace to accept with serenity the things that
>   cannot be changed,
> courage to change the things that should be changed,
> and the wisdom to distinguish the one from the other.

This version of the poem-prayer as quoted by Elizabeth Sifton, daughter of theologian Reinhold Niebuhr, to whom it is often attributed, caught the eye of Bill W. more than sixty years ago, and in a slightly different version, became *the* mantra of Alcoholics Anonymous. Long and short versions of the prayer have been found in Celtic and Far Eastern spiritual practices, and in most languages on earth. As Bill W. wrote, "Never had we seen so much A.A. in so few words."

> *God grant me the serenity to accept the things I cannot*
> *   change,*
> *courage to change the things I can,*
> *and the wisdom to know the difference.*

"In creating A.A.," Bill wrote, "*The Serenity Prayer* has been a most valuable building block—indeed a cornerstone." This poetic cornerstone is a perfect example of spiritual connection.

Poetry is the most honest verbal expression among any people, at any time, in any situation. It comforts and challenges reader and writer alike. Contemporary poet Allen Grossman calls poetry "the historical enemy of human forgetfulness" and attributes to it the capacity of self-preservation. Poetry's meditative power in spiritual practice awakens you and makes you more skillful as you navigate life's rapids. It connects you to me and others. Through poetry, you also carry on the two most intimate conversations of your life—the conversation with your Supreme Being and that with yourself.

Poetry as spiritual practice leads to stillness, the calm center where you are most open and alive. Poetry itself makes you more mindful, and as you become so, you gracefully reconnect with the natural world. Through poetry as spiritual practice, you become a more confident communicator and a more attentive, compassionate listener. Mindfully using applications of poetry can create patience and greater harmony among friends, in families and professions. As you hear or speak poetry, the particles in your brain connect and dance, creating physical sensations of lightness, darkness, joy, and sorrow. Through poetry's sound and pictures, its cadences and imagery, you achieve greater awareness and more intimate knowledge of things seen and unseen and more abundance in your spiritual life.

Nothing creates greater understanding of poetry and intimacy with it than writing it yourself. Writing poems opens windows, doors, and opportunities. You can write in solitude—in a bedroom, a parked car, on a plane or train, in a cubicle at work, on a mountainside. You can write with a group—a spiritual community, a reading club, a writing workshop, and with friends as you hang out. Anyone who is compassionate, who yearns for deeper awareness, and who possesses the human gift of language has the innate ability to write poems.

In other words, everyone can write poetry. You don't need special knowledge or a graduate degree in literature. Spiritually, all you need to bring to the table is a willingness to be open; practically, you need to know that poetry is written in lines, not sentences, which conform to the breathing of its creator rather than to the artificial signposts of punctuation marks and conventional grammar.

A poem's lines are usually organized in stanzas instead of paragraphs (prose poems, which we'll explore later, are an exception). A poem may rhyme and move in a traditional meter, or exist in the measured rhythms of free verse. A poem employs figurative language such as metaphor and simile, assonance and dissonance, and vivid imagery to stimulate the senses and illuminate meaning. A poem compresses meaning and is rigorously concise. A poem may be a song, a meditation, or a story.

In the chapters that follow, we'll explore the sound and language of poetry, its building blocks, rhythms, meters, and forms. You'll keep a working journal of your reading, your thoughts and poems. You'll challenge yourself with concise, pleasurable writing exercises, including some provided by well-known poet-mentors such as Mark Jarman, Diane Thiel and R. S. Gwynn. We'll examine the genres of elegy, free verse, narratives (poems that tell stories), and eight traditional poetry forms. You'll write your own poems in these forms and discover how these and other poems fit into and deepen your spiritual practice.

As a poet, editor, and teacher, I took decades to learn what the pages that follow reveal. I knew that poetry and spirituality were somehow sympathetic, but I had trouble connecting the dots in order to use poetry confidently in my spiritual practice. Then a few key factors converged, leading to my breakthrough.

In 2004, I moved away from my religious roots in Catholicism and became a student of Tibetan Buddhism, embarking on a daily Ngöndro (pronounced "nundro") practice.

A Tibetan term meaning "that which precedes or goes before," Ngöndro refers to the basic practices of all four schools of Tibetan Buddhism and paves the way for advanced practices, which may ultimately lead to realization and enlightenment. The Ngöndro practice I follow includes a series of mantras, prayers, visualizations, prostrations, offerings, and meditations that can take from twenty or forty minutes to an hour or even the entire day.

As I was beginning this new path, I read about a requirement in medical schools that has since become widespread: that medical students take courses in poetry and creative writing so that they develop more empathy for their future patients, learn how to draw patients into telling their own stories, and listen well to details and to what patients imply in their choice of words. These exchanges between doctors and patients promote healing. It struck me that, if poetry can aid physical healing, perhaps it can also promote spiritual healing. Medical schools that teach poetry are in fact asking their students to develop greater compassion and meditate on their patients' lives. This sounds very much like a spiritual agenda or *practice.* Many Buddhist prayers and mantras are in fact poems, such as those by the monk Milarepa, so, since reading about the healing effect of poems and prayers, I've consciously included more poems and prayers in my own daily practice.

For example, recently I was feeling terribly frustrated about my country's conduct in the Middle East. I recited a poem I knew three times and felt calmer and sadder, but also more patient and hopeful. Here is the poem:

Paper Cranes

How can we tell a paper bird
Is stronger than a hawk
When it has no metal for talons?
It needs no power to kill
Because it is not hungry.

Wilder and wiser than eagles
It ranges round the world
Without enemies
And free of cravings.

The child's hand
Folding these wings
Wins no wars and ends them all.

Thoughts of a child's heart
Without care, without weapons!
So the child's eye
Gives life to what it loves
Kind as the innocent sun
And lovelier than all dragons!

I love the defiant joy of that final exclamation point! The poem, by the late Trappist monk Thomas Merton, was inspired by members of a visiting peace group whom Merton received at Gethsemane, the Kentucky monastery where he lived, in May 1964. At the end of the visit, one smiling, silent woman, a Hiroshima survivor, placed a folded paper crane, a Japanese symbol for peace, on his table. Like that appropriate, inspired gift, the poem restores perspective as it woos the ear through meter, rhyme, repetition, and potent imagery. It helped me to become more profoundly understanding, patient, and compassionate, and it knocked my well-intentioned moral superiority out of me.

Including poems in my daily meditations and prayers intensifies my experience and enriches my results. Though it may not always appear to be true, spiritual practice done over and over again bears fruit. If I think diligently about loving kindness and forgiveness, and on bestowing them on individual people I know and even on people I don't know, I will become kinder and more compassionate.

Emily Dickinson wrote, "If I feel physically as if the top of my head were taken off, I know that it is poetry." I think again of my friend who liked the way poetry made him feel physically, even though he did not know that *The Prayer of Saint Francis* was poetry. You can feel that, too, as you discover poetry in your spiritual practice and weave it into the fabric of your daily life.

Virginia, an Englishwoman I met recently, managed to do just that. Her mother, orphaned when she was six and raised by Catholic nuns, had kept Virginia as far away from the Catholic church as she could. When Virginia was old enough to go

to church, her mother took her to the neighborhood Luther-
ans. A reluctant churchgoer, Virginia was finally baptized there
when she was thirteen. After that, she attended services irregu-
larly, and when her mother died a week before her seventeenth
birthday, she stopped going altogether.

Virginia was twenty-six and married by the time she suf-
fered a miscarriage and was diagnosed with leukemia. The
burden of irreparable loss and fatal illness lifted somewhat
when she began to attend morning mass at the Catholic church
across the street from her home.

"I got the irony," she told me. "My mom was so spooked by
anything Catholic, and there I was stumbling into mass every
day! I don't know what it was. Sitting in that almost-dark felt
good. I liked looking up through the stained-glass windows. I
didn't pay any attention to the figures on the windows. I just
liked the light, the colors. I got into the sound of Mass, too, all
that chanting."

The parish priest, Father Patrick, visited Virginia at home
twice a week, and they discussed God, heaven, and all of the
spiritual questions Virginia could think of. Father Patrick sug-
gested that Virginia try meditation as part of her prayer prac-
tice, which she did. But she was frustrated, not sure that she
was getting it or getting anything out of her attempts. When
she told Fr. Patrick what she was going through, he introduced
her to a friend of his, Ani Una, a nun (Ani means "nun") who
studied Buddhism and had been meditating for twenty years.
Naturally, Virginia wanted to know how Una got meditation
to work for her.

"Not easily," the sister laughed, "not at first. I was frustrated,
too, like you. Then I began to add poems to my recitations
and something good started to happen. I included all kinds of

poems—serious, sad, even light and funny. Those were especially good because they reminded me that my practice should be joyful, not drudgery. I wondered why the poems worked in me like they did. It was the words in their sequence, and the meaning of the words. Both took me deeper into whatever I was working on—letting go of things I was attached to, lapses of faith, unkind acts or words. Poetry doesn't lie! Poems make me feel . . . like nature itself, like a blade of grass. They make me feel as if I could climb water!" Three months later, Virginia told Una that she was also including poems in her practice, and they were helping her find peace, a connection with God, and a spiritual sense of healing and fulfillment.

That's my wish for everyone who experiences this book.

One

The Shape of Practice, the Mystery of Poetry

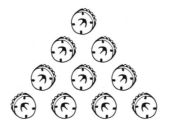

1

Clearing Obstacles:
Joyful Rituals of Poetry as Practice

Once you reconnect with poetry, realizing that in fact it has been a part of you since you were conceived, it's easier to rest in its company. From there you can work with it. But as you contemplate poetry as spiritual practice, consider, for the next few moments, how and why poetry may have frightened you.

A few years ago, I chaired a panel at the Northwest Book-fest in Seattle that engaged in a lively discussion with audience members about the perception that poetry turns a cold shoulder toward the general reader, that many who write it seem to be uninterested in communicating to a wide audience. One of the panelists, the poet Thomas Lux, agreed and said, "We have to stop writing poems that make people feel stupid."

Has poetry ever made you feel stupid? Self-conscious? Have you thought less of yourself in certain company after admitting that you like poetry?

In practical, earthly terms, what good *is* poetry? Having confessed that you like it, have your friends accused you of being highfalutin? Did your parents disown you? Did you lose your job or fail in your studies? Did your partner dump you? Did you walk down the street slump-shouldered and blushing while everyone laughed and pointed at you? Probably not. Your fears are almost always scarier, more dramatic, than the actual course you must run.

Exercise: Facing Your Fear

Before you can break through to a state of centered grace from which the spiritual practice of poetry is possible, you must make a friend of your fears about poetry. You must make your fear a good teacher. Here is a poem about fear, anxiety, and poetry by Cyrus Watson, a twenty-nine-year-old workshop student:

Bud & Night Terrors

Can't let them catch me!
If my parents find out I'm writing poems
They'll cancel Christmas. No Nikes, no Play Station III,
No kick-butt pants with twenty miles of chains on them.
They'll empty my college fund, certain I'll never be
The doctor or lawyer they want me to be. Worse,
Coach will kick me off the team, or knock
Me down to towel or water boy. My minister will
Unbaptize me, my Boy Scout pack will rescind
My merit badges, the Marines will get me
Though I'm only 17! All because of poetry.
What got into me? Why wasn't watching ten hours
Of TV a day good enough for me? *Why?*

Does this poem sound like something you have thought, like something you might have written once? Make a list of your own poetry fears. Share your list with friends. Discuss where they come from. How do you deal with them? Why should you? Be specific! Write your own poem poking fun at your poetry fear.

Exercise: "It's Alive! It's Alive!" What Is It?

First, make a list of your own definitions of poetry. Second, seek the opinions of others by asking people you know (spiritual mentor, family, friends, the grocer, the crossing guard, the librarian, your doctor, your coach, your employer, the barista at Starbucks). Meditate on these definitions. Discuss them with friends, which will give you an opportunity to read a friend's heart. What common ground can you discover among people with different spiritual beliefs, education, jobs, reading, and entertainment habits?

Exercise: Personal Pyramid

Visualization is always useful. Construct a personal pyramid of poetry, a pyramid that presents all of the reasons you've discovered to back up the fact that poetry is important to you. For example, the cornerstones of my personal poetry pyramid are Honesty and Community. From your own cornerstones, erect the pyramid using ten blocks in all, with four blocks as your foundation, three blocks across above it, two blocks in a shelf above that, and one block as your pyramid's tip. For example:

Intention

Character   Witness

Imagery   Spirituality   Memory

Honesty   Music   Humor   Community

Because we are all connected, you may use some of my pyramid parts, but you might place them in different positions. That's appropriate. All pyramids are valid, and all of them can change.

Share your pyramids. They're an opportunity to open up to each other. Discuss what you've learned about listening, truth, and prioritizing your concerns. How have the pyramids under discussion added to your expectations? Your writing and spiritual goals? It's insightful to revisit your pyramids from time to time, for they accurately depict your transformative journey. Tending them reminds you where you've been, where you really are, and where you may wish to go.

Collaborative Exercise: Poetry Pros and Cons

Team up with a friend and prepare a five-minute dialogue, with one of you taking a position defending poetry as spiritual practice, and one of you taking the opposite view. You could imagine that you are the host of a radio program interviewing your friend. Each of you should come up with three reasons for the point of view you represent. Discuss what you discover through this modeling/rehearsing. Your friend might argue, for example, that poets make things up or even lie; therefore, they are inappropriate spiritual mentors or guides. Or you might argue, as W. H. Auden once did, that poetry, spiritual or otherwise, makes nothing happen. Another argument you might make? Poetry makes us more compassionate.

Here is a poem by Gretchen Fletcher of Florida about writing poetry:

Fishing

It all starts with a line
whisked from behind
the head, flung far out
across the shoulder to hover
over a pregnant stream
before breaking the surface and sinking,
sinking till thumb-stopped
and set with a backward crank.
Then down there in that black world
a midge-sized feather of an idea
goes to work, looking,
looking for something to use—
some prism-scaled trout, perhaps,
that will land flapping at our feet,
gasping our air with vermillion gills.
Even some ancient algaed boot
Will do, home to worms and leeches,
tailing long untied strings
and strands of water weeds.
Then the process starts
All over with the casting,
casting about for something
to write about line after line,
to the last line.

In this poem, Fletcher suggests that fishing and writing require supreme patience, a giving in to process. The practitioner must discover satisfaction not so much in the end result, but in the act of doing. This requires faith, and all who have faith are really quite brave, are they not?

Here is another poem about poetry. This one is by Dori Appel of Ashland, Oregon.

The Management of Poems

Sometimes you need to outsmart them—
when they lapse into a silent sulk
or become too reasonable or
get puffed up with their cleverness.
Occasionally, they imagine they've
arrived through divine inspiration
and sashay through the house
embarrassing everyone, or they go on
a jag with the family albums,
lamenting dead hamsters they never
got to say goodbye to, pissing and
moaning their old regrets.

Those are the times to leave them
to themselves, and go pull weeds.

In this poem, the author's relationship to the writing of poems seems adversarial, even exasperated. Haven't we all been there? In fact, this poem is itself a metaphor for its author and her obstacles. As in the Fletcher poem, Appel comes to the realization that great patience is needed, but that sometimes the best way to achieve patience (and complete a poem) is to walk away, to rest, regroup, and redirect energy until the inevitable return to the task. This poem is really a lesson in detachment, in letting go.

Both of these poems, like many other poems about poetry, chronicle a writer's starts and stops. They bear witness to the poem's quicksilver nature, to the writer's frustration and humility. Perhaps most important, they share the *experience* of making poems and celebrate poetry itself.

David Chase, the creator and producer of the HBO series *The Sopranos*, was asked in an interview to describe the formal distinctions between his show and shows on network television.

"Network television is all talk," Chase said. "I think there should be visuals on a show, some sense of mystery to it, connections that don't add up. . . . There should be, God forgive me, a little bit of poetry."

David Chase is nearly right. There should be poetry in everything. But not just a little bit. There should be a lot, and there is. There is poetry in every aspect of our daily lives. We worry that poetry is not useful. We fear it is not practical, that it will somehow turn others against us, that it will impede our day-to-day progress. We are afraid that poetry will somehow get in the way of our life plans.

Yet once we open ourselves anew to poetry, remembering perhaps how sacred poetry defined our earliest moments and experiences, once we retrain our faculties, we discover that we are richer in every way. President John F. Kennedy understood poetry's importance when he wrote, "When power leads man toward arrogance, poetry reminds him of his limitations. . . . The artist . . . becomes the last champion of the individual mind and sensibility against an intrusive society. . . ."

Once you've neutralized your poetry fears, once you've cleared away your personal obstacles and opened yourself to the promise of a spiritual practice blessed by poetry, you may very well ask yourself, *How? How do I proceed?* It's an appropriate question at such a life-turning moment, and it may be answered best by considering the processes of some notable writers.

John Keats, the great English poet who died at age twenty-six in 1821, prepared to write poetry by taking a bath. Afterward, he would dress in his finest clothes, peel and slice an apple, and pour a glass of good red wine. Placing the apple slices and the wine glass just so on his desk, he would sit down, dip his quill in an ink pot, and begin to write.

Despite the fact that he was poor and dying of tuberculosis, Keats wrote until he was too sick to sit up or move his pen across paper. His writing ritual sustained Keats to the end of a brief life in which he never lost the desire to analyze his deepest insights and feelings and communicate them to those close to him, and those who might one day read his verses and letters. On some important, divinely human level, illness did not matter. Even though he would not live long enough to share a life with the woman he loved, he created enduring communication, poems we read and feel and learn from even today. Here is the inspiring conclusion of his long poem *Sleep and Poetry:*

> . . . from off her throne
> She [poetry] overlooked things that I scarce could tell.
> The very sense of where I was might well
> Keep Sleep aloof: but more than that there came
> Thought after thought to nourish up the flame
> Within my breast; so that the morning light
> Surprised me even from a sleepless night;
> And up I rose refreshed, and glad, and gay,
> Resolving to begin that very day
> These lines; and howsoever they be done,
> I leave them as a father does his son.

Poetry's surprise, its ability to restore us, making us feel "refreshed, and glad, and gay," is also the gift it gives our spiritual practice.

John Keats shared with all people the desire to find in life the spiritual intimacy that creates successful community and makes living a fully awake life so worthwhile. As a poet, Keats certainly responded to urgency, as in real time rapidly running out, as in recording his words just so, as in making memorable language that both worries and wins over the ear, as well as the heart and mind connected to the ear. He succeeded by reuniting poetry and spirituality, by opening himself up, by attending to detail, which we may assume is a skill he acquired as a medical student. Shaping words into pentameter ballads, sonnets, brief lyrics, and gorgeous meditations, Keats created forms of sound and idea that ring true to this day.

Where's the Poet?

Where's the poet? Show him! show him,
Muses nine, that I may know him!
'Tis the man who with a man
   Is an equal, be he king,
Or poorest of the beggar-clan,
   Or any other wondrous thing
A man may be 'twixt ape and Plato.
   'Tis the man who with a bird,
Wren or eagle, finds his way to
   All its instincts. He hath heard
The lion's roaring, and can tell
   What his horny throat expresseth,
And to him the tiger's yell
   Comes articulate and presseth
On his ear like mother-tongue.

Emily Dickinson grew up and lived all her life in Amherst, Massachusetts, when that village was one of America's first cultural centers. Hers was a prominent family, but not so much so that they were set apart from general Amherst life. Dickinson herself was a petite, vivacious girl and woman, probably disappointed in love, definitely a protofeminist, always capable of discovering surprise in the world and being surprising herself. In her drab, long-sleeved dresses, with her hair tied back in a tight bun, she would burst into conversation that must have startled listeners, at times, like heat lightning in a distant summer sky. Bristling with nervous energy, fearful that she would not be able to control herself and thus offend someone, in later years she would sometimes talk to visitors from around the corner of the second-story landing while remaining out of sight.

She wrote wonderful, lively letters, thousands of them, to family members and close friends, and she wrote poems, strange, magnificent verses that stutter, soar, and pierce like no poems ever written before, or since. Growing up under the influence of Ralph Waldo Emerson's grand philosophical thought, Transcendentalism, Dickinson also learned by heart the effective formal style of New England hymnals (again, poetry as the language of exultation, of prayer), before giving up going to church in her teens. Even so, few poets have ever so diligently and brilliantly braided together poetry and a spiritual practice. Poems were Dickinson's prayers, her mantras.

Poem #949

Under the Light, yet under,
Under the Grass and the Dirt,
Under the Beetle's Cellar
Under the Clover's Root,

Further than Arm could stretch
Were it Giant long,
Further than Sunshine could
Were the Day Year long,

Over the Light, yet over,
Over the Arc of the Bird —
Over the Comet's chimney —
Over the Cubit's Head,

Further than Guess can gallop
Further than Riddle ride —
Oh for a Disc to the Distance
Between Ourselves and the Dead!

I adore the nimble balance in this poem of yearning. The poet strives to see the intricate, mysterious connections between people and the rest of the natural world, and between the living and the dead. By capitalizing nouns, by starting every line but the last one with an emphatic, stressed syllable, she instills in her query an urgency that sweeps us up and feels exhilarating. Who wouldn't want to burrow and soar like . . . well, like angels!

Surely Emily Dickinson aimed to *say it right* and *be heard.* Of her success with the former, there can be no doubt; the latter goal mostly proved elusive in her lifetime. But after her death at age fifty-seven, her sister discovered in her dresser neatly hand-sewn packets of more than 1,700 poems. Though she published only seven poems during her life, it is inconceivable to imagine her living without the daily companionship, the daily discoveries she found in her poetry. It is equally hard to believe that she did not care if her poems ever reached a wide audience. Today a worldwide community, surely larger than Dickinson ever imagined, communes through her poems with her formidable, inspiring spirit.

Poem #1151

Soul, take thy risk,
With Death to be
Were better than be not
With thee

This is poetry as spiritual practice. Though we will never meet the poets we've met here in person, they're available to us as inspiring mentors and spiritual friends. They lift us out of ourselves, transcend self-interest, and make life more meaningful and fun.

In his book *The Mastery of Love*, the *nagual* from the Toltec Eagle Knight Lineage, Don Miguel Ruiz, speaks of the "shock that stops love little by little over time." Specifically, he is talking about a moment when a child is surprised by the actions of a fearsome mother. The child, who is interested only in *now*, in happiness and play, is hurt by what he perceives as an uncalled-for punishment. The punishment diminishes the child's innocent awareness, his natural freedom. Poetry recalls and embodies that natural freedom. It restores our connection to innocence. But most of all, poetry is created out of love, which never survives in a vacuum. It springs from the unquenchable desire to learn, to connect with others, to process and transform loneliness. Even if no one ever reads my poem, I imagine someone in the room with me, listening, benefiting. Communicating, after all, is intrinsic to the poet's calling.

Exercise: Eavesdropping

This activity can be done virtually anywhere. All it requires is good listening and note-taking. It can be a great icebreaker, a way of overcoming writer's block.

Go to a public place like a coffee shop, bookstore, or gym. Listen to the conversations going on around you. Record one or more. Later, construct a poem out of them. This exercise will simply get you started, and you will learn something about handling dialogue in a poem. The next day in your spiritual practice, recite the poem you wrote while generating compassion for the strangers you listened to.

Collaborative Exercise: Cutting Up

Exchange poems with a partner. Take scissors in hand and cut up your partner's poem (while your partner does the same to yours). Rearrange the lines to make a new poem. A variation: put the cut-up lines in a hat, then draw them out one line at a time. The result is your new poem. You may learn something about the random aspects of inspiration and the lucky or happy gift that writers dream about. This exercise may also be useful in developing the practice of letting go of attachments to negative emotions and past experiences that impede living wholly in the moment.

The exercise we have just done delivers us to another question about poetry, and another potential obstacle. The question? Why isn't poetry prose? It's not a silly question at all! Professional writers sometimes ask it, too. Some critics and teachers even argue that there *is* no difference, but there is. A cat's tail, after all, is not spaghetti. An apple is not an orange. A Toyota is not a Jaguar.

There is a simple difference between poetry and prose, and

here it is. The delivery system of all prose is the sentence, while the delivery system of poetry is the line. The rhythms of sentences differ from the rhythms of lines of poetry. We breathe differently when we read a sentence aloud or in our heads than we do when we read a line of poetry. The difference between the two is physiological and imaginative.

Those who doubt this claim should consider the late, great Raymond Carver. Why did Carver, universally recognized as our modern master of short fiction, bother to write poetry at all? He won fame and made money, a lot of it, writing fiction, but he wrote poetry early on and all through his life because he recognized that verse allowed him to discover things and say things that prose did not. Specifically, as a man recovering from an addiction that was almost fatal several times, he found in poetry a spiritual practice that aided his program.

What Carver knew, and what many have found as well, is that lines of poetry manage and present the passage of time in ways that prose sentences do not. Poetry is more concerned with timelessness and less with literal or fractured sequence. Poetry is more capable of associative leaps and makes greater use of the power of suggestion. Its primacy in our rituals proves that poetry is accessible communication, not code. Ultimately, poetry distills emotion, experience, and even location in ways that would feel unsatisfying in a novel or creative nonfiction. Poetry aims to say what absolutely must be said, and in the fewest possible words.

A poem wants to realize and offer up, no matter how loud or quiet, a rhythmically ordered moment of powerful emotional discovery. It wants to separate itself from the business and busyness of prose. For example, consider Walt Whitman's beautiful twenty-two line poem, *Out of the Cradle Endlessly*

Rocking. The poem is in fact a single sentence, but it works in our ears and hearts because it is measured out in lines. This is the magic of rhythm in poetry.

> Out of the cradle endlessly rocking,
> Out of the mocking-bird's throat, the musical shuttle,
> Out of the Ninth-month midnight,
> Over the sterile sands and fields beyond, where the child
>   Leaving his bed wander'd alone, bareheaded, barefoot,
> Down from the shower'd halo,
> Up from the mystic play of shadows twining and twisting
>   As if they were alive,
> Out from the patches of briers and blackberries,
> From the memories of the bird that chanted to me,
> From your memories sad brother, from the fitful risings
>   And fallings I heard,
> From under the yellow half-moon late-risen and swollen
>   As if with tears,
> From those beginning notes of yearning and love there
>   In the mist,
> From the thousand responses of my heart never to cease,
> From the myriad thence-arous'd words,
> From the word stronger and more delicious than any,
> From such as now they start the scene revisiting,
> As a flock, twittering, rising, or overhead passing,
> Borne hither, ere all eludes me, hurriedly,
> A man, yet by these tears a little boy again,
> Throwing myself on the sand, confronting the waves,
> I, chanter of pains and joys, uniter of here and hereafter,
> Taking all hints to use them, but swiftly leaping beyond them,
> A reminiscence sing.

This is an ecstasy of rhythm, an exquisite bouquet of devotional form. In twenty-two lines, Whitman demonstrates what it means to be a poet, a "chanter of pains and joys." Emily Dickinson surely would have said that this poem satisfies her definition of verse: "If I feel as if the top of my head were taken off, then I know it is poetry."

An insight like Dickinson's provokes deeper investigations into ourselves, the nature of poetry, the making of poetry, and what it does for us. But at other times, insights like it can be discouraging. Sometimes we feel that an accomplished poet confounds us as much as the mysteries of life itself.

No writer of poetry escapes feeling this discouragement many times, just as no serious spiritual practitioner denies encountering many disturbing bumps in the path. How often have you caught yourself thinking, *I cannot write a poem, I don't know what to say*, or *I practice and practice but never feel profoundly different*, or *I'm just not getting anywhere in my spiritual practice!* All of us experience these doubts and frustrations, and when we do, we're being tested. Through such adversity we learn perseverance, patience, humility.

It is no different when we write poems. In any pursuit, it's natural to feel, at times, a personal futility, a sense that all of the work worth doing has already been done. Anyone who has ever played baseball marvels at the effortlessness in the performance of even the most marginal major leaguer, but that grace is a product of commitment and endless repetition, endless learning. It is a result of taking thousands of practice swings and ground balls in order to train the mind and body to achieve that artful illusion of simplicity. The most renowned spiritual teachers have suffered and overcome breathtaking doubt. All poets, even the greatest who ever lived, have experienced moments of profound futility. For all of us, the time comes when it's inevitable to think, *Why bother?*

The answer is not a riddle. The answer is that our divine energy compels us to work and play. It is our nature to work, to practice. It is essential that we play. As thinking, spiritual beings, we are compelled to focus and direct our abilities, to bring them to bear on chosen and appointed tasks. We thrive on teasing out the intricately wound skein of experience and natural laws. Because we also have feelings, we must open ourselves more deeply to the spiritual journey, to relationships with ourselves and others.

We can learn to write and read poetry as a valuable aid to this process. We can learn to share poetry, its beauty, wisdom, and lessons, with others. In doing so, we enhance our abilities in our chosen life paths, our work. Most important, we wake up to poetry's essential part in our spiritual practice. At that moment, it is as if a long-settled cloud in our mind suddenly lifts, and we are divine once again.

Poetry opens up a thrilling lifelong dialogue, self to creator and self to self, that makes possible greater understanding of who we are, and of how we responsibly create and care for community. Poetry makes us better listeners, wiser talkers. Poetry is tolerance, understanding, empowerment. Poetry is practice, *spiritual* practice.

God's-Acre

I like that ancient Saxon phrase, which calls
    The burial-ground God's-Acre! It is just;
It consecrates each grave within its walls,
    And breathes a benison o'er the sleeping dust.

God's-Acre! Yes, that blessed name imparts
    Comfort to those who in the grave have sown
The seed that they had garnered in their hearts,
    Their bread of life, alas! no more their own.

Into its furrows shall we all be cast,
    In the sure faith, that we shall rise again
At the great harvest, when the archangel's blast
    Shall winnow, like a fan, the chaff and grain.

Then shall the good stand in immortal bloom,
    In the fair gardens of that second birth;
And each bright blossom mingle its perfume
    With that of flowers, which never bloomed on earth.

With thy rude ploughshare, Death, turn up the sod,
    And spread the furrow for the seed we sow;
This is the field and acre of our God,
    This is the place where human harvests grow.

(Henry Wadsworth Longfellow)

Exercise: Poetry to Prose

Take one of your poems and turn it into one or two paragraphs. Add or delete words and punctuation as needed. How does rhythm and intention change?

Exercise: Prose to Poetry

Select a meaty paragraph from a contemporary novel. Using its sentences as a diving board, rewrite the paragraph in lines, adding or subtracting words and punctuation as needed. Does the meaning change? What about the rhythm? What has been gained or lost, or both?

Collaborative Exercise: Two Ways of Telling the News
With a partner, research and compose paragraphs that report a compelling news story. Next, tell the same story as a poem. Imagine Bob Woodward and Carl Bernstein cracking the Watergate scandal wide open in a poem. Again, what is gained or lost?

2

Nursery Rhymes, Chants, and Hymns:
Early Encounters with Poetry as Practice

The sun and moon
Are coming soon
To breakfast with their fiddles.
Get out of bed
You sleepyhead
And eat my healthy vittles.

*

God says be good
God says be good
God says be good
Or else!
Be bad he says
Be bad he says
Be sad, a low louse.

All of us recall simple chants from our earliest days. Some of them haunt us, some amuse us, and some still seem mysterious and strange. One I still remember vividly followed me every day in 1960 on my way to and from second grade.

Kids delighted in taunting each other with "Nixon's at the White House waiting to be elected! Kennedy's in a garbage can waiting to be collected!" Naturally, children from Democratic households simply reversed the order of the proper names, but either way it quickly became exasperating!

Shards of simple poetry like those above lodge in our physiology, as do even earlier poetry experiences. Our mother's rhythmic breathing, heartbeat, and physical rhythms, which we know in the womb, are our earliest experiences of poetry, which are soon followed by lullabies and nursery rhymes or chants. These vocal patterns bond caregiver and child, help children become social beings. Here, for example, are several Mother Goose rhymes you'll recognize.

Rock-a-bye, baby,
In the tree top:
When the wind blows,
The cradle will rock;
When the bough breaks,
The cradle will fall;
Down will come baby,
Cradle and all.

Many of us associate the rhyme above with Mother's voice, or perhaps an older sister's or aunt's, as she sang it while putting us to bed.

Monday's child is fair of face,
Tuesday's child is full of grace;
Wednesday's child is full of woe,
Thursday's child has far to go;

Friday's child is loving and giving,
Saturday's child works hard for its living;
But the child that is born on the Sabbath day
Is bonny and blithe, and good and gay.

This poem taught us the days of our week, though the declaration about Wednesday's child (I am one!) seems rather bleak and unfair; the next poem taught us how to memorize the days in each month.

Thirty days hath September,
April, June, and November;
February has twenty-eight alone,
All the rest have thirty-one,
Excepting leap year, that's the time
When February's days are twenty-nine.

*

Hey! diddle, diddle,
The cat and the fiddle,
The cow jumped over the moon;
The little dog laughed
To see such sport,
And the dish ran away with the spoon.

This last rhyme taught us the magical joy of words in unusual combinations, perhaps our first encounter with metaphor. Do you recall the sheer delight you felt when you first heard this rhyme and saw with your mind's eye the images it describes?

Exercise: Back to the Nursery

In your journal or notebook, write a short series of rhymes in the spirit of Mother Goose. Let your rhyme-horse out of the corral to run free! Remember: nothing is incorrect. You may be as unpredictable as you wish. Just have fun. Write on any subject. Write about yourself as a parent or write about your child. Describe your room, your car, your office. Be uninhibited. Have fun!

Chants and nursery rhymes teach us early in life that spiritual awareness happens anywhere, at any time. As musician and writer Robert Gass reminds us, "We can chant in the car while commuting to work, chant in the shower, chant while preparing food or cleaning the house, even while opening junk mail." Like Gass, many have discovered that chanting can be a form of meditation that calms the mind and cuts through mindless chatter. It transforms our prayers into music and song, into poetry itself. Jewish cantors chant and sign centuries-old prayers to inspire the congregation, which lifts up its voice in praise of and in conversation with God. Tibetan Buddhists chant through a practice called throat singing, in which notes vibrate in a series of frequencies to make the mind still. Indeed, all of the world's religions include chants.

Unlike nursery rhymes and chants, hymns are specifically written to contain simple or elaborate prayers. The Greek *hymnos* means "a song of praise." The ancients all over the world composed hymns. Hinduism produced a famous collection of hymns, the Vedas. The pharaoh Akhenaten wrote the *Great Hymn to the Aten*:

How manifold it is, what thou hast made!
They are hidden from the face (of man).

O sole god, like whom there is no other!
Thou didst create the world according to thy desire,
Whilst thou wert alone: All men, cattle, and wild beasts,
Whatever is on earth, going upon (its) feet,
And what is on high, flying with its wings.
The countries of Syria and Nubia, the land of Egypt,
Thou settest every man in his place,
Thou suppliest their necessities:
Everyone has his food, and his time of life is reckoned.
Their tongues are separate in speech,
And their natures as well;
Their skins are distinguished,
As thou distinguishest the foreign peoples.
Thou makest a Nile in the underworld,
Thou bringest forth as thou desirest
To maintain the people (of Egypt)
According as thou madest them for thyself,
The lord of all of them, wearying (himself) with them,
The lord of every land, rising for them,
The Aton of the day, great of majesty.

In this hymn, the pharaoh praises the Sun God for creating the earth, nurturing the crops and animals, and rescuing all from the terrors of the night. Compare it to the cadences of the King James Bible's first verses of Genesis and their version of Creation:

In the beginning God created the heaven and the earth. And the earth was without form, and void; and darkness was upon the face of the deep. And the Spirit of God moved upon the face of the waters.

And God said, Let there be light: and there was light.

And God saw the light, that it was good: and God divided the light from the darkness.

And God called the light Day, and the darkness he called Night. And the evening and the morning were the first day.

And God said, Let there be a firmament in the midst of the waters, and let it divide the waters from the waters.

And God made the firmament, and divided the waters which were under the firmament from the waters which were above the firmament: and it was so.

And God called the firmament Heaven. And the evening and the morning were the second day.

And God said, Let the waters under the heaven be gathered together unto one place, and let the dry land appear: and it was so.

And God called the dry land Earth; and the gathering together of the waters called he Seas: and God saw that it was good.

Western hymnody begins with the Homeric Hymns, which praised the gods of Greek mythology. Christian hymns, originally modeled on the Psalms of David, were defined by Thomas Aquinas as "the praise of God with song; a song is the exultation of the mind dwelling on eternal things, bursting forth in the voice." Modern westerners who attended church or other organized religious services experienced poetry as spiritual practice in a communal, formal setting. If you doubt this, consider this familiar hymn:

> Silent night! Holy night!
> All is calm, all is bright
> round yon virgin mother and child!
> Holy infant so tender and mild,
> sleep in heavenly peace!

How about this one?

> Hark! The herald angels sing,
> "Glory to the new-born King;
> peace on earth and mercy mild,
> God and sinners reconciled!"
> Joyful all ye nations rise;
> join the triumph of the skies;
> with the angelic host proclaim,
> "Christ is born in Bethlehem!"
> Hark! The herald angels sing,
> "Glory to the new-born King!"

In fact, the earliest known poem in English was written to be sung. Only a fragment remains, which is called *Caedmon's Hymn.*

According to the historian Bede, Caedmon lived in the seventh century and worked in the stable of a monastery. He had never composed poetry before, but one night in a dream

a man commanded him to sing for the monks and other work-
ers. When the shy mucker said that he could not sing for so
many, the man instructed Caedmon to sing for him alone.
Puzzled, Caedmon asked what he should sing about and was
told to sing about the creation of all things. When he awoke,
Caedmon had composed a passionate hymn of praise. When
he performed it at dinner that night, the monks believed his
song was a gift of God's grace. Only nine lines still exist, and
here they are in their native Old English, followed by the mod-
ern English translation.

Nu scilun herga hefenricaes uard
metudaes mehti and his modgithanc
uerc uuldurfadur sue he uundra gihuaes
eci dryctin or astelidae
he aerist scop aeldu barnum
hefen to hrofae halig sceppend
tha middingard moncynnaes uard
eci dryctin aefter tiadae
firum foldu frea allmehtig

Now let me praise the keeper of Heaven's kingdom,
the might of the Creator, and his thought,
the work of the Father of glory, how each of wonders
the Eternal Lord established in the beginning.
He first created for the sons of men
Heaven as a roof, the holy Creator,
then Middle-earth the keeper of mankind,
the Eternal Lord, afterwards made,
the earth for men, the Almighty Lord.

The connection between hymns and poetry has never confused or surprised a hymnodist or poet, who is aware that hymns are actually poems set to music. One common way we talk about a hymn is to identify its meter, which allows the hymn to join together lyrics and meter. Today we commonly identify thirteen hymn meters, and here is one, part of Reformation leader Martin Luther's *A Mighty Fortress Is Our God:*

> A mighty fortress is our God, a bulwark never failing;
> Our helper He, amid the flood of mortal ills prevailing:
> For still our ancient foe doth seek to work us woe;
> His craft and power are great, and, armed with cruel
>   hate,
> On earth is not his equal.
>
> Did we in our own strength confide, our striving would
>   be losing;
> Were not the right Man on our side, the Man of God's
>   own choosing:
> Dost ask who that may be? Christ Jesus, it is He;
> Lord Sabaoth, His Name, from age to age the same,
> And He must win the battle.

With its unusual five-line stanzas, this hymn is in P.M. or Psalm Meter (we will explore meter in greater detail in Chapter 6), which can also be referred to as Peculiar Meter because of its nonstandard use of stressed syllables. For instance, there are seven stressed syllables in lines one and two, six in line three, seven in line four, and three in line five.

Another example is *Amazing Grace* by the hymnist and abolitionist John Newton.

Amazing grace, how sweet the sound
That sav'd a wretch like me!
I once was lost, but now am found,
Was blind, but now I see.
'Twas grace that taught my heart to fear,
And grace my fears reliev'd;
How precious did that grace appear,
The hour I first believ'd!
Thro' many dangers, toils and snares,
I have already come;
'Tis grace has brought me safe thus far,
And grace will lead me home.
The Lord has promis'd good to me,
His word my hope secures;
He will my shield and portion be
As long as life endures.
Yes, when this flesh and heart shall fail,
And mortal life shall cease;
I shall possess, within the veil,
A life of joy and peace.
The earth shall soon dissolve like snow,
The sun forbear to shine;
But God, who call'd me here below,
Will be forever mine.

This beautiful song is composed in C.M., or Common Meter. The first line includes four stressed syllables, the second line three stresses. Lines alternate in this way throughout the hymn, as do the simple rhymes. Lines one and three rhyme, as do lines two and four, and so on.

Amazing Grace is such a powerful hymn that it has even crossed cultures. The Cherokee nation translated and sang it repeatedly along the infamous Trail of Tears. As tribal members died on the arduous forced march, survivors were not allowed adequate time to bury the dead. The singing of the hymn accompanied the grievous rushed internments, its poetry providing some comfort in cruel circumstances. Here in alternating lines is the Cherokee translation of *Amazing Grace.*

u ne la nv i u we tsi
God's Son
i ga go yv he i
paid for us.
hna quo tso sv wi yu lo se
Now to Heaven He went
i ga gu yv ho nv
After paying for us.

a se no i u ne tse i
Then He spoke
i yu no du le nv
when He rose.
ta li ne dv tsi lu tsi li
I'll come a second time
u dv ne u ne tsv
He said when He spoke

e lo ni gv ni li squa di
All the world will end
ga lu tsv he i yu
when He returns

ni ga di da ye di go i
We will all see Him
a ni e lo hi gv
here the world over.

u na da nv ti a ne hv
The righteous who live
do da ya nv hi li
He will come after
tsa sv hna quo ni go hi lv
In heaven now always
do hi wa ne he sdi
in peace they will live.

It's significant that the earliest recorded poem is also a hymn intended for spiritual practice. Poetry in the form of rhymes, chants, and hymns helps practitioners from an early age and throughout life to articulate spiritual lessons and celebrate spiritual truths, and it helps practitioners of all faiths. I encourage anyone who doubts that poetry is the speech of God, of the infinite, of a superior power, to listen to recordings of Paul Robeson singing hymns and African-American spirituals.

Examples of spiritual poet-practitioners from diverse religions and beliefs are plentiful. Rabia of Basra, the most revered Islamic female saint, who lived and wrote almost five hundred years before the better-known (in the West) Rumi, created chants for her practice:

Slicing Potatoes

It helps me, working my hands in a pot,
swishing a broom in a wash pail.

I tried painting,
but I took flight far more easily
by slicing potatoes.

Rabia's earthy imagery invites immediate connections to our own experience. Her message? Working humbly and well gets better results than grandiose flights of fancy. Rabia also wrote a useful chant about troublemakers:

Who Really Knows Anything About God?
I know. Many think they do,
but they're just troublemakers!

Tukaram was an unschooled yet immensely influential mystic poet in seventeenth-century India. He, too, delighted in composing chants to augment his spiritual practice.

Because I could not lie
I named my dog "God."
Startled at first,
Soon he was smiling
Then dancing!
Now he won't even bite.
Do you suppose this might work
On people, too?

*

Shell Game

God slipped into
One of your pockets.
Now you can always find Him!

Tukaram even delights in writing inspiring bolts of words about poetry.

There's a hole in the palace wall.
A good poem is like that!

You never know what you might see.

Mirabai, a woman saint and poet of India, whom we met briefly in the Introduction, wrote chants, hymns, and songs that Hindus and Muslims recite to this day. Here is one about the divinity of women:

God delights in women,
for they hold the world
to their breasts
and help Him comfort.

Exercise: Your Hymn

Imagine what it must have been like to be Caedmon. You're naturally shy, and every night, after a long, grueling day of labor, you must eat dinner with fellow workers and monks while everyone around the table takes turns singing. It sounds like an introvert's worst nightmare! There you are at table, cringing, dying inside as you await the inevitable tapping on your shoulder as a monk says it's your turn, get up and sing. Imagine escaping for a night, for a week, as so many sing and you are overlooked, or there is simply not enough time for everyone. Still, you know your time will come. Then what? Then, in a dream, you find a voice and words you never knew before. Where did they come from? What do they signify?

What are they for? Now, *be* Caedmon. In your notebook, write about the creation of all things. You don't need to repeat what you've read in the Bible, or what you've heard or been told. What comes to your clear mind when you read the words 'the creation of all things'? Write Dana's Hymn, or April's Hymn, or Avi's Hymn. It's your hymn, your divine song. Open up your heart and sing your grace note, if only to yourself.

Chants and hymns are forms of address and forms of group communication. They give us an opportunity to make more concrete and immediate our musing about life's meaning and life's events. They are forms in which we may sum up our investigations, tell what we know, and communicate across time and space. They may be lessons of instruction or simple attempts at humor. Often they are expressions of a practitioner's humility and devotion, celebrations of the Divine in all of its diversity and deliciousness.

Exercise: Chants of Your Own
Referring to the models we've just met (or remet) above, write your own chants that celebrate, reflect on, or seek divine response in your own practice. Practice fearlessness and write the precious words that only you know. They're the devotional, insightful words already inside you.

Always chants are poetry, laying the groundwork for poetry's presence in everything we think, feel, and do throughout life. From the womb to death itself, poetry works its magic in our energy fields whether we know it or not. There is so much more benefit, and so much more fun, to knowing it and working it!

3

The Shape of Practice:
Waking Up Through Poetry

As I began to realize that poetry could enrich and deepen my spiritual practice by sharpening my attention and more clearly defining my goals, I was puzzled by this question: what would praying a poem look like? I'd read and written poetry and loved it most of my life, but how would praying it work, how would it feel? Perhaps more important, was it appropriate? Certainly, I did not want to be willfully or ignorantly sacrilegious! Poetry as spiritual practice was an intriguing idea, but I was strongly tempted to maintain my comfort level, to go on, as it were, reciting prayers and chants, and singing hymns in church without giving a lot of thought to what I was really doing and saying.

Yet in truth I was not very comfortable and felt restless, in need of something new to help and inspire me. But I resisted change. I chose to stay put because—well, because that's what I knew! But I wasn't happy, and I was aware that something was missing. Of course, what was missing was the music and meaning of beautiful words, the breakthrough experience of divine utterance.

Reawakening to this truth (for I'd known it as a child but had forgotten it), I also saw that I needed to figure out how to use poems in a spiritual way. Spiritual practice requires focus and harmony. It wasn't good enough to recite poems I happened to like, skipping around like a dilettante. I was stuck for a time, but succeeded in breaking down how I best learn something important. As a child, I learned how to pray, sing, and honor my elders; as a teen, I learned how to drive a car; in school, I learned math, science, history, and languages. In these and all of the other examples of learning I could recall, I realized that there was one common denominator—a mentor!

Learning any skill—spiritual skills, poetry skills, life skills—is made possible and enhanced by mentorships that affect us even when we are not wholly aware of them. Consider how you learned to get up in the morning. If the alarm or radio station failed, you could count on a parent, sibling, or roommate to goad you out of bed. Almost certainly you resented it, but the intervention usually made you grateful later on.

Mentor-apprentice relationships can also shape and sustain spiritual and temporal practice, and they exist in the body of poetry like capillaries in the body of a human being.

Mentoring and apprenticeship have always been central to spiritual practice. Lamas, gurus, priests, pastors, rabbis, teachers, and parents are indispensable mentors. Jesus, Muhammad, Buddha, and their most celebrated interpreters mentor us through their teachings.

One such figure is Saint Francis, who is so revered for his compassion that thousands of non-Catholics place his statue in their gardens. But Francis had once considered forsaking his monastic life and faith because he could not overcome his revulsion at the sight of lepers. Wrestle though he might with his shame, whenever he saw a leper, he panicked and ran the other way. He would literally run! This is not the image of Francis that the world reveres today.

Francis's faith crisis tormented him for a long time until one day, while he was walking down a country lane toward a village, a leper staggered through the hedgerow and stood in his path. Francis froze, but this time he did not run. Instead, he embraced the poor man and kissed him full on the lips. At that moment, not when the church decreed it so many years hence, did Francis attain sainthood, the state of complete identification with and compassion for another's suffering and the recognition of the goodness or inherent divinity in that other person.

Mentor-apprentice relationships are not exclusive to humans, for they're common in the natural world, too. I'm fond of this very old folk story as an illustration.

A family is trapped when a portion of the roof of the cave they're exploring collapses. The family members despair at ever digging their way out, worry about having enough air, and worry about dying of thirst. As they chip away at the wall of rock that confines them, they suffer many irrational, bleak moments. Taking a break, one of them discovers that they are not alone in the cave. A large tortoise has been keeping them company.

The family continues to dig, but as the hours pile up, their thirst becomes maddening. Then the daughter witnesses something amazing. A single drop of water falls from the ceiling above the tortoise, but before it can hit the ground, the tortoise's tongue darts out and catches it just so. The tortoise's tongue retracts, and its wise eyes seem to say to the girl, "That is how you may survive. Slow down, be patient, learn everything you can about your surroundings. Observe. Work steadily. Be ready."

The tortoise mentors the family in survival, and eventually they dig their way to freedom. It's significant that the mentoring comes from a nonhuman source, for that fact spiritually reconnects the human beings in this story with the natural world.

Natural-world mentoring is common in stories of spiritual quests in our daily lives. The McCormicks, authors of the highly recommended *Horse Sense and the Human Heart* and *Horses and the Mystical Path: The Celtic Way of Expanding the Human Soul*, provide several moving tales of horses providing humans with wise spiritual counsel.

One that haunts and inspires me involves an old, prized stallion, the beloved elderly patriarch of a valuable herd (in Central Europe?) during World War II that appeared to be doomed by the imminent occupation of advancing Nazis. The stallion's owner, also elderly, had no way to transport his horses to safety, but if they could somehow be led hundreds of miles through difficult mountain terrain, they would reach a safe haven. The old man doubted that the plan would work, as there were not enough hands to keep the horses together, and there would be little food or water along the way. Despairing, the old man went out in the evening and talked to the stallion for hours. He explained their dilemma. In the end, not knowing what else he could do, he simply asked for the horse's help.

The next morning, the stallion led the other horses out of their corrals and, despite his advanced years, calmly led the entire herd to safety, after which he lay down and died. But his spirit and courage lived on in his offspring and other members of the group he had saved.

Shaping spiritual practice requires effort, and work itself is an honorable spiritual activity. Poetry's role in this work can determine in large part the depth and range of practice, for it is poetry that most deliciously sharpens the senses, heightening awareness and presence in the moment. An earnest apprentice quickly grasps this connection between poetry and spiritual practice. Just looking around us with real attention, we see mentor-apprentice relationships everywhere.

Mountain climbers, shoemakers, physicians, and carpenters must serve serious apprenticeships before they become accomplished in their fields. The architect Frank Lloyd Wright created his own academy with twenty-three original live-in apprentices who learned to prepare raw materials for buildings; they also collaborated on cooking, housework, and gardening. In 1917, Louis Armstrong began a two-year apprenticeship to King Oliver, the master of New Orleans jazz. The late Bruce Lee served as a brilliant mentor to a whole generation of apprentices in the martial arts, and his influence is seen to this day in breathtaking, choreographed martial arts scenes on film and TV. The actor, radio personality, and director Orson Welles made a film that is generally regarded as the greatest of all time, *Citizen Kane*, when he was twenty-six years old. When asked how he learned to make movies he replied, "By studying the masters. John Ford, John Ford, and John Ford." In other words, the elder director Ford, through his own memorable films, acted as a mentor to the apprentice Welles.

All writers I've ever known or heard of served important apprenticeships. Mark Twain and Geoffrey Wolff apprenticed as newspaper reporters. A teenage Ernest Hemingway apprenticed himself as a reporter to the editors and beat writers at the *Kansas City Star*. The newspaper trade taught them, and many other writers, to write to deadlines, adhere to word limits, produce readable copy for various assignments, learn to edit, and polish sentences. Newspaper writing also teaches writers that composition is not always pure inspiration, that good writing can be the result of dogged determination and hard, joyous work.

The point is, spiritual work is everywhere in our lives, not simply in the recitation of prayers and mantras. Spiritual practice is more than ritual. It's being in the wisdom moment when the mind and heart are wide open to learning and love.

The apprentice works to master a practice, craft, or trade, but what of the mentor?

"Mentor" was originally the name of a Greek character in *The Odyssey* who was an elderly friend of Odysseus's and tutor to his son, Telemachus. Mentors help an apprentice learn a craft or way of life and an apprentice helps them, too, to produce their work or legacy. The teachers you have known throughout your formal education have all, on some level, answered the call of mentoring and believe in passing on their wisdom and knowledge.

Julia Cameron, author of *The Artist's Way: A Spiritual Path to Higher Creativity*, had a spiritual, writerly mentor all of her early life in her grandmother, though she did not realize it until later. Her grandmother lived to be eighty and regularly wrote "long, winding letters" about her life to her granddaughter. To Cameron, they were "like a long home movie: a shot of this and a shot of that, spliced together with no pattern that I could ever see."

Eventually, Cameron saw that "life through grandma's eyes was a series of small miracles: the wild tiger lilies under the cottonwoods in June; the quick lizard shooting under the gray river rock she admired for its satiny finish." She saw that her grandmother persevered by "standing knee-deep in the flow of life and paying close attention." Even though her mentor-grandmother died before Cameron truly learned the lessons those letters taught, she left behind in them a record of experience (and experiencing them again and again itself became valuable experience) that schooled Cameron in her own life. In time, Cameron learned from those letters that "survival lies in sanity, and sanity lies in paying attention." They taught her that "the truth of a life really has little to do with its quality. The quality of life is in proportion, always, to the capacity for delight. The capacity for delight is the gift of paying attention." That's exactly what mentors give to their apprentices.

Nothing is too small or insignificant in mentor-apprentice relationships. John Wooden, the greatest college basketball coach of all time (his UCLA Bruins won an unprecedented and unmatched ten NCAA titles in twelve years), developed over his long career a Pyramid of Success that includes fifteen steps to achieving your best results in anything you choose to do. Wooden taught his young men not just to be superior players, but to be well-rounded, successful, and beneficent human beings. No detail escaped his attention. For example, Wooden knew that a player's feet endure incredible punishment over a long season. So, at the beginning of every new year, he would teach each player the proper way to put on his socks. Does this seem trivial, even silly? In fact, it's brilliant in its simplicity, and Wooden's results were spectacular. Nothing is insignificant for one who would be wide awake. As the author and life coach Brian D. Biro has pointed out, "the mind is like a parachute; it functions best when it is open." These coaches are bodhisatt-vas, a saintlike practitioner of Buddhism and compassion, whose actions benefit other beings.

My own mind has been opened by spiritual mentors like Father Pat Walsh, many years ago, and recently Lama Bruce Newman, author of *A Beginner's Guide to Tibetan Buddhism*, who helped me to concentrate my effort and better understand my goals in practicing, and by worldly mentors who also imparted spiritual wisdom.

When I was sixteen, I talked myself into a job as a reporter for the *Monterey Park Progress*, a local newspaper in Southern California. The fastest two-fingered typist on an Underwood I've ever seen, Johnny Edwards, was my editor. He looked like the classic Hollywood newsroom character with his rumpled white shirts, the sleeves rolled up. Puffing on a cigarette that seemed to live in his face, he gave me special assignments and made me rewrite my articles over and over. I had just about had enough when one day I walked into the office and was greeted by my latest effort on the front page of the paper. It was the first time I thought of myself as a professional writer. Thanks to Johnny Edwards, I gained much-needed skills, validation, and confidence. I saw that I should be more demanding of my writing and myself, and began to see how to edit myself to become even better.

In my undergraduate years at the University of California at Santa Cruz, I was lucky to receive mentoring from Raymond Carver, David Swanger, and the poet, playwright, actor, novelist, and editor of *Kayak* magazine and press, George Hitchcock, who became a lifelong mentor. Hitchcock's lessons are many, and still sustain me, and I'll share one that changed the course of my life.

In one Hitchcock workshop, a small group of my new poems appeared on the worksheet for class critique. After I read them aloud, my peers applauded my effort. I basked in their affection, swooned to their cheerleading. Nobody said a negative word. At last, it was Hitchcock's turn.

"I could take the best one or two lines from each of these poems and make one really good poem," he said.

The air left the room. It spurted out of my swelled chest. My mentor said what he'd said without malice or delight. He said it as if it were true, as if it were something I needed to hear. I felt a surge of anger that I struggled to control. Still simmering in my room late that night, I looked down at my poems, and I saw that George was right. I had been too easy on my words and myself. I had figured out that my peers would be entertained and kind. I had settled for less. At that moment, Hitchcock's tough love provided just the lesson I needed.

That year, I got a summer job working the graveyard shift at Salz Tannery in Santa Cruz. Tanneries are noisy, smelly, scary places, and the one I found myself at six days a week was no exception. I started out doing odd jobs—stirring lye baths, sweeping, stacking pallets, emptying trash. Two weeks after I'd been hired, a foreman told me that one of the four fleshing machines had opened up. Would I be interested in taking on the job? When he told me I'd earn five dollars an hour more than I was making, I knew all I needed to know to say yes. At least I thought I knew.

Fleshing machines are exactly what they sound like—huge devices designed to cut the last layer of flesh off a half-hide, which weighs on average 150 pounds. The operator stands on a platform and operates the fleshing machine by foot pedals— one to open its maw, one to close it. Turning his back on the machine, the operator bends down to pick up a half-hide from a pallet delivered by forklift. Lifting the hide, he turns in a half circle, lays half of it across the giant roller, hits the CLOSE pedal with his foot as he turns, and receives the cleansed half of the hide as it feeds out from the ever-rotating cylinder blade. Then he opens the maw, flips the hide to cleanse the other half, and repeats the process. When the hide is fully stripped, he pauses halfway through his three-quarter circle back to the pallet to toss it into a waiting bin. This process is repeated on average a thousand times in a seven-hour shift.

It was grueling, terrifying work, and it was even worse once I learned that the man I'd replaced had slipped on his greasy platform and instantly lost an arm up to his shoulder to the whirring blade. I might very well have met with a similar fate if Titus, a beautiful African-American man of about forty-five and a nine-year operator of fleshing machine number one, had not taken me under his wing. With fatherly goodwill and kindness, Titus schooled me in the fierce machine I had to operate. He showed me the tricky footwork required, how to lay the hide across the roller so that the blade would not spit it out, or worse, yank at it, pulling the operator with it. He taught me how to flip hides, pace myself, even how to conduct myself in the break room. Without Titus, I doubt that I would have lasted a week. With him, I actually became a valuable fleshing machine operator.

A very different act of mentorship affected me greatly in graduate school during a writing workshop led by the poet Richard Eberhart. Eberhart was in his seventies then, an established, generous author and teacher. One night, he and his wife, Betty, invited me to their apartment at the Chelsea Hotel. We talked poetry late into the night. At some point, I confessed my passionate devotion to the poetry of Emily Dickinson. Eberhart smiled and extended his hand. I hesitated, not knowing what I should do. His hand remained extended to me. I reckoned I should shake it, and did.

"Congratulations," he said. "Now you can always say that you shook the hand that shook a hand that held the hand of Emily Dickinson."

Eberhart explained. As a young man in New England he became friendly with an old woman. Discovering that Eberhart was a poet, she told him that she had been one of the neighbor children in Amherst who gratefully received Emily Dickinson's baked goods from her own hands. With a simple gesture and anecdote, Richard Eberhart had mentored me in the passage of time, the links between generations, and the encoding of flesh to flesh.

Over the years, I've enjoyed collecting other writers' stories about mentors; here are a couple of my favorites.

Rita Dove, a Poet Laureate of the United States, wrote her first poem as a little girl. Her subject? The Easter Bunny. The poem's rhyme and meter made it easier for the young writer to recite, which she was called on to do many times as she grew up in Akron, Ohio. Those recitations may have temporarily satisfied in the child poet the desire to find community through writing, a desire so strong it also led her to writing and producing, with friends and siblings, a newspaper that was then distributed around the neighborhood. Several teachers in grade school and high school helped Dove become the writer she is today, and she has always been vocal about her gratitude.

Some forty years later, when she became Poet Laureate of the United States, Dove continued to champion the expression of traditionally underrepresented community voices by organizing readings at the Library of Congress featuring high school students from Indian reservations and readings featuring poets from many cultures abroad.

All along, Dove has maintained a dual career as a writer and a teacher of writing. These callings are driven by an urgency to serve others. It's the urgency that sparks dynamic cross-talk between people who might otherwise remain isolated, and ultimately powerless, without it. Like her childhood teachers, Dove has become an inspiring mentor for a new generation of young people.

Another poet, Jetsun Milarepa, whose life bridged the eleventh and twelfth centuries, was one of Tibet's most famous yogis and is generally acknowledged as the first to attain Vajradhara (complete enlightenment) within a single lifetime.

Milarepa's early life hardly fit the profile we imagine for an enlightened being. Born to a prosperous family but disinherited by his uncle and aunt when his father died, Milarepa studied sorcery, which he used to murder dozens of people and destroy crops as he exacted his and his mother's revenge.

Haunted by his actions, Milarepa apprenticed himself to the stern lama Marpa the Translator. Perhaps because Milarepa's past was so dark, perhaps because he was headstrong, wanting quick results, Marpa refused to teach him until the supplicant built a tower. Milarepa did so, and Marpa ordered him to destroy it and build another. Milarepa erected and destroyed three towers, left in despair to begin to study meditation with another guru, and only returned to Marpa when he was told he would never make any progress without Marpa's blessing. Milarepa studied diligently for twelve years with his master until, at the age of forty-five, he became a wandering teacher with Marpa's blessing.

Milarepa's experience gives us a particularly arduous example of apprenticeship. Of course, most of us will never experience apprenticeships as extreme as Milarepa's under his mentor Marpa, but then the extremity of the experience is not the point. Every mentor-apprentice relationship is unique, with the mentor creating a course of study that will most effectively benefit the apprentice. The proof of the relationship's success is evident in the apprentice's work and practice later on.

Here is an excerpt from a poem by Milarepa that is generally referred to as *The Song of View, Practice, and Action.* Despite its address to Buddhist practitioners, this poem is encouraging and useful to anyone who is interested in shaping a spiritual poetry practice. All religions, for instance, contain versions of the Ten Virtues and Ten Vices, the Dharmakaya (lessons, or scripture), Nirvana (enlightenment) and Samsara (this sinful, suffering life). The poem is in fact Milarepa's blueprint for shaping spiritual practice. Certainly, Milarepa believes in and practices the primacy of poetry in his own hard-won practice, and he demonstrates by doing that we can do the same.

> Oh, my Teacher! The Exemplar of the View, Practice, and
> Action,
> Pray vouchsafe me your grace, and enable me
> To be absorbed in the realm of Self-nature!
>
> For the View, Practice, Action, and Accomplishment
> There are three Key-points you should know:
>
> All the manifestation, and Universe, is contained in the
> mind;
> The nature of Mind is the realm of illumination
> Which can neither be conceived nor touched.
> These are the Key-points of the View.

Errant thoughts are liberated in the Dharmakaya;
The awareness, the illumination, is blissful;
Meditate in a manner of non-doing and non-effort.
These are the Key-points of Practice.

In the action of naturalness
The Ten Virtues spontaneously grow;
All the Ten Vices are thus purified.
By corrections or remedies
The Illuminating Void is ne'er disturbed.
These are the Key-points of Action.

There is no Nirvana to attain beyond;
There is no Samsara here to renounce;
Truly to know the Self-mind
Is to be the Buddha himself.
These are the Key-points of Accomplishment.

It is one of the great spiritual truths that mentor lessons never leave us, even long after the mentor is gone. And then, one day, if we are fortunate, we find ourselves passing them on, assuming the role of mentor for someone else. This exchange occurs among the living and between the living and the dead.

Here is a poem by Maxine Kumin about tuning in to a mentor she never knew in her own life. But she knew the woman well through her art and the example of her life. Kumin's poem is also, brilliantly, about the very nature of poetry which, she says, "is like farming." In this simple simile, Kumin says all one might need to say about poetry as spiritual practice.

A Calling

Over my desk Georgia O'Keeffe says
I have no theories to offer and then
takes refuge in the disembodied
third person singular: *One works*
I suppose because it is the most
Interesting thing one knows to do.
O Georgia! Sashaying between
first base and shortstop as it were
drawing up a list of all the things
one imagines one has to do . . .
You get the garden planted. You
take the dog to the vet. You
certainly have to do the shopping.

Syntax, like sex, is intimate.
One doesn't lightly leap from person
to person. *The painting*, you said,
is like a thread that runs
through all the reasons for all the other
things that make one's life.
O awkward invisible third person,
come out, stand up, be heard!
Poetry is like farming. It's
a calling, it needs constancy,
the deep woods drumming of the grouse,
and long life, like Georgia's, who
is talking to one, talking to me,
talking to you.

I wrote a poem to honor a mentor, Frederick Morgan, a year after his death. The poem is an elegy, a genre we'll work with in a later chapter, but it is also a celebration of our mentor-apprentice relationship, which began in 1977 and continues to this day through his published books and the memory of the many things he taught me. I can still hear Fred's voice, the art and joy of his conversation. Once a mentor's voice is inside you, it's always there to be listened to; it adds depth, wisdom, and artfulness to your own voice.

Talking with the Dead

Morning. Ocean rain and fog.
I wake uneasy in the Gold Beach motel,
Scratching in my brain to set the day right
And here it is, the calendar reminding me
That on this day a year ago you died.

On this day a year ago you packed
Your gentle manner and disarming clarity,
Your kindness and bawdy humor,
Your high pitched laugh and pixie face
And crossed over, leaving the phone dead,

The crowded dining room hollow,
The reservoir iced over, the lovers ashen,
The tennis courts deserted.
Ever since I've wanted to get even
With Death. I've wanted to bring you back

Where you belong—a purely selfish act
If I could pull it off. I've wanted to join you,

Loving your company, happy where you were.
Your exit knocked me off my stride,
A rhythm I can't seem to find again.

The Left Behind can't help but make it all about them.
We wade in shadows for answers we can't have,
And though we never left a word unsaid,
I'd give a world to sit with you and talk
Just as we used to do. Now it's in my head,

The work of keeping you alive. Just as you
Constantly renewed yourself (and have again,
for all we know), I keep your lesson close:
Be open, honest, true; be rigorous and loyal,
But most of all be joyful in everything I say and do.

The world is shining even as we lose
The people, things and scenes we cherish most.
Walking on the beach, my son whose middle name
Is yours collects stones and makes up stories for each
    one.
A life can be a model. I learned that much from you.

Here are some exercises to help you find mentor influences
in your own life, which can help you find or reclaim a spiritual
practice as well as contribute to reflections that can inspire
your own poetry writing.

Exercise: Witness Mentors and Apprentices at Work
Meditate on the nature of mentor-apprentice relationships.
Consider how mentors help you learn about listening, about

being open and present in the moment. Focusing on others around you, make a list of mentor-apprentice relationships you have observed. Write about their dynamics in your journal, or discuss them with your reading, writing, or meditation group. One or more of these relationships may suggest a promising topic for a poem. Make a reverent effort to write it.

You may also enjoy doing a little research into significant mentor-apprentice relationships in literature or history (some of which were cited earlier). Make a list of half a dozen to share and discuss with people in your reading or writing group, or with a group of spiritual practitioners, then choose one example and write three or four paragraphs, or a poem, about it. Think primarily about how the things the apprentice learned from the mentor ended up shaping the apprentice's life and work.

Exercise: Personal Experience I

After completing your daily prayer or meditation, move your attention to the living mentors to whom you have apprenticed yourself in your life. Make a list of them, short or long. Now write a paragraph describing each one, and the things you've learned from them.

Next, meditate on occasions in your own life when you mentored someone. Write paragraphs describing each one, including what you learned from each incident. Describe what you believe you taught your apprentices.

Now, write your own tribute to each of these roles, each of these experiences, in prose or poetry. The point is to get in touch with the spirit of these friends, teachers, parents, or others who inspired you.

Exercise: Personal Experience II

Our mentors are not bound by life or death. We need not know someone in the flesh to be taught by them—or to teach them! Repeat the steps presented in the first half of *Personal Experience I* above, but this time think of mentors who have had an important effect on your life whom you've met through your reading or in stories you've heard.

Collaborative Exercise: Be a Mentor; Be an Apprentice

Team up with someone who will mentor you in a skill she or he possesses. When you have achieved some basic mastery of the skill, reverse roles. How does this new knowledge and skill enhance your poems and practice?

For instance, a few years ago I met a new mentor in the award-winning author and cook Rebecca Wood. Attending my first evening class in her home with eight other people who wanted to learn how to cook healthier meals, I realized that I'd begun an exciting, beneficial new apprenticeship. I've observed Rebecca's spiritual nature come through in everything she does. She is so mindful in the way she speaks to individuals, the way she cocks her head with a sweet smile as she listens without ever breaking eye contact. Her compassion shines like a halo around her as she serves others by preparing and serving delicious, nurturing food. Most significant, however, is the cadence of her speech. Her sentences are imagistic and compressed. They say what needs to be said, and they say it beautifully, concisely. Combining spiritual practice and avid reading, Rebecca often naturally speaks in the cadences of poetry. Her poetic speech and life of good-hearted service are an inspiration to me in my own practice as a teacher and poet.

Two

Building Blocks

Records

Another
Russian
has returned
after
2,000,000
miles
in orbit.

Today I sat
motionless
for
28
minutes
while a
butterfly
folded its
trembling
wings
and rested
on my knee.

(George Hitchcock)

4

Words, Metaphor, Simile

Without words, a poem is as parched as land without water. Our words, fueled by playfulness and inspiration, morph into figures of speech, expressions we can't get out of our heads. As children, we take delight in creating oddball rhymes and contradictory combinations of words. One of my favorite made-up words, for instance, is *mangry*, a combination of *mad* and *angry*. It's a fun word because it covers craziness, spontaneity, and simmering rage.

No one was more inventive or had more fun with words than Lewis Carroll, the creator of *Alice in Wonderland*. His famous nonsense poem, *Jabberwocky*, never grows dull:

'Twas brillig, and the slithy toves
Did gyre and gimble in the wabe:
All mimsy were the borogoves,
And the mome raths outgrabe.

"Beware the Jabberwock, my son!
The jaws that bite, the claws that catch!
Beware the Jubjub bird, and shun
The frumious Bandersnatch!"

He took his vorpal sword in hand:
Long time the manxome foe he sought—
So rested he by the Tumtum tree,
And stood awhile in thought.

And, as in uffish thought he stood,
The Jabberwock, with eyes of flame,
Came whiffling through the tulgey wood,
And burbled as it came!

One, two! One, two! And through and through
The vorpal blade went snicker-snack!
He left it dead, and with its head
He went galumphing back.

"And hast thou slain the Jabberwock?
Come to my arms, my beamish boy!
O frabjous day! Callooh! Callay!"
He chortled in his joy.

'Twas brillig, and the slithy toves
Did gyre and gimble in the wabe:
All mimsy were the borogoves,
And the mome raths outgrabe.

Despite its nonsense, we delight in this familiar tale of a boy defeating a monster. Of course, the monster is immaterial. What matters is that the boy faces and overcomes his fears. The made-up words make us smile and enjoy the experience even more.

As figures of speech in poems, words become our building

blocks. Nouns (words that name things) and verbs (words that create action, movement) are generally more dynamic and effective in poems than other words such as adjectives (words that modify nouns and pronouns), and adverbs (words that modify verbs, adjectives, and other adverbs). Poems include these types of words as well, but the most successful poems rely on nouns and verbs, which are more like your immediate family as opposed to distant relations.

The Pool

Are you alive?
I touch you.
You quiver like a sea-fish.
I cover you with my net.
What are you—banded one?
      (H.D.)

Words in a poem must be figuratively and emotionally appropriate. We expect to find a higher incidence of metaphor and simile, alliteration and assonance, in poetry than in prose. It's the figurative language of poetry that makes possible our inner transformation.

Figurative language enables us to envision and describe our spiritual practice as a journey. Yet while we may not be going anywhere physically, our spirits are traveling a long way. In this sense, we're acting out a small drama in the spirit of metaphor. Similarly, on approaching a bridge, you think of it as the beginning of the crossing, but when you retrace your path and cross back, you don't think of it as the end; how can a segment of the bridge be both beginning and end? Yet it makes perfect sense because metaphorical thinking allows us to see that it is so. Metaphorical thinking comes naturally to us, and the greatest teaching and learning are transmitted through metaphor. For example, medical intuitive and spiritual teacher Caroline Myss sees individual, personal illness and spiritual challenges reflected in the global environment; it is not surprising, she says, that cases of drug-resistant pneumonia and tuberculosis have increased as the destruction of the rain forests—the Earth's lungs—has increased, or that the general weakening of the human immune system is mirrored in the Earth's damaged ozone layer, its protective shield.

"Metaphor," writes the Canadian author J. Edward Chamberlin in his book, *If This Is Your Land, Where Are Your Stories?* "is the basic trick of language, and we are sometimes impatient with tricksters. But the door between reality and the imagination can't do without a hinge." All metaphors and similes are riddles, hinges combining one thing with another. They are contradictions, asking us to see a thing as it is and as it is not. Yet the thing is always the thing itself. "Taking metaphor seriously," Chamberlin reminds us, "brings us face to face with the most subversive act of language."

Metaphors and similes often join together essentially unlike things to demonstrate an underlying connection. In *How to Read a Poem: And Fall in Love with Poetry*, poet Edward Hirsch writes that "the poetry of love has always been enamored by comparisons, haunted by issues of similitude." He cites the *Song of Songs*, in which "the lovers vie with each other in their praise for each other. (Love poets have competed for the most extravagant comparisons ever since)." In fact, all poets are in love with comparisons. They allow a writer to present description in vivid, surprising detail that transcends argument and logic.

Examples of metaphor can include:

The Lightning is a yellow Fork/From Tables in the sky . . .
  (*The Lightning is a Yellow Fork,* Emily Dickinson)

His car is dumb and warm.
  (*Indian Boarding School: The Runaways,*
  Louise Erdrich)

Her thoughts are drones/serving a terrible queen of
  their own.
  (*Battle of Will & Exhaustion, Mother & Child,*
  Jenny Factor)

Examples of simile include:

The Nerves sit ceremonious, like Tombs—
  (*After Great Pain, a Formal Feeling Comes,*
  Emily Dickinson)

I was of three minds,
Like a tree in which there were three blackbirds.
  (*Thirteen Ways of Looking at a Blackbird,*
  Wallace Stevens)

The squat pen rests, snug as a gun.
  (*Digging,* Seamus Heaney)

Comparisons that inspire a sense of wonder, then greater
understanding, are essential to spiritual practice and a cul-
ture's self-awareness, its sense of history. In Native-American

cultures, for example, the landscape *is* the body; the body *is* the landscape. This is metaphor in its most vital and elemental form. Here is an Apache poem-prayer addressed to the mountain spirits:

> Mountain Spirit, leader of the Mountain Spirits, your
>   body is holy.
> By means of it, make him well again.
> Make his body like your own.
> Make him strong again.
> He wants to get up with all of his body.
> For that reason, he is performing this ceremony,
> Do that which he has asked of you.
> Long ago, it seems you restored someone's legs and eyes
>   for them. This has been said.
> In the same way, make him free again from disease.
> That is why I am speaking to you.

Similes are more obviously balanced than metaphors, as both sides of the comparison are explicitly stated. As Chamberlin puts it, "the *like* is a foot in the door, or maybe the trickster's hinge." Metaphors act more quickly, relying as they do on a reader's ready ability to grasp the unstated, unknown, or unexpected. A metaphor makes an immediate transformation, saying that one unlike thing *is* another; the simile teases more ambiguity into the equation, suggesting that one unlike thing is *like* another thing. Distance is inherent in simile but not in metaphor. The reader encountering a simile has a split second longer to ponder, to make a connection, then leap.

Of course, one must be wary of inappropriately mixing figures of speech, as in a mixed metaphor (*Niall took a mighty swing with the wind*—a bat, even by a long, generous stretch, cannot be made of wind). Here is another example of inappropriate figurative language: *Then, like the burning bush, the grocery list erupted in mother's hand.* It is inappropriate to compare a symbol of religious significance to something as mundane as a grocery list.

Equally ineffective are dead metaphors. *I think that I shall never see/A poem lovely as a tree* is an example of a dead metaphor, or what the philosopher-poet Ralph Waldo Emerson called a fossil metaphor. The comparison of a poem to a tree is tired. There is no surprise and no magic in it.

Neither metaphor nor simile operates on the literal plane. As Edward Hirsch has pointed out, "when Henry James describes a house, he is also describing the inhabitants of that house." Metaphors and similes are not farm animals in a pen. They are not colorless, toneless, or shackled by judgment and assumptions. They are not the thing itself, but the thing itself *and* itself.

Exercise: Identifying Metaphors and Similes
Identify metaphors and similes in the examples that follow.

1. Hell-mouth is a head
   Like a boulder in the dirt, bald and well-fed.
     (*The Heavenly Ladder of John Klimax*,
     Mark Jarman)

2. The yellow fog that rubs its back upon the window-
   panes . . .
     (*The Love Song of J. Alfred Prufrock*, T. S. Eliot)

3. I am the arrow.
   (*Ariel*, Sylvia Plath)

4. The only sanity is a cup of tea.
   (*Boy Breaking Glass*, Gwendolyn Brooks)

5. Love me like a wrong turn on a bad road late at night.
   (*Like That*, Kim Addonizio)

6. He came home as quiet as the evening.
   (*Youth*, James Wright)

7. The city unpeels like a plotless movie.
   (*Towers of Silence*, David Mason)

8. Inside the veins there are navies setting forth.
   (*Waking from Sleep*, Robert Bly)

9. This poem is the reader & the reader this poem.
   (*beware: do not read this poem*, Ishmael Reed)

10. And you're east of east saint louis
    and the wind is making speeches,
    and the rain sounds like a round of applause . . .
    (*Time*, Tom Waits)

Exercise: Metaphors and Similes on Your Own
Make up a list of twenty metaphors and another list of twenty
similes of your own.

Exercise: Metaphor and Simile in Your Practice
Make a list of all of the metaphors and similes you can find in your regular spiritual practice. Take them out of your practice, and note how it feels and sounds without them.

Exercise: Bad Figurative Language
Make a list of ten mixed metaphors and ten fossil metaphors. (Hint: politicians are delightful and exasperating fountains of mixed metaphor; advertising can be a fecund source of fossil metaphors.) Share these with your friends. Just for fun, make a poem using as many of them as you can. Don't be shy. You can bust through your blockages in learning by being bold enough and free enough to laugh at yourself.

Collaborative Exercise: Group Metaphors and Similes
Select one of your best metaphors and one of your best similes. Borrow one of each from a good friend. Using these two metaphors and similes, write a poem of your own. The borrowing in this exercise makes poetry a communal art. Even its making need not be wholly solitary. In some ways, your peers are also your mentors.

5

Alliteration and Assonance

lliteration and assonance are ways in which a poet emphasizes and enriches consonants and vowels. They create agreement between like sounds within a line or stanza. Most of us are actually quite familiar with the effects of alliteration and assonance. Familiar phrases like "high as a kite" and "mad as a hatter" (assonance), or "luck be a lady" and "loose lips sink ships" (alliteration) owe their ongoing popularity in large part to the magic of alliteration and assonance.

Nursery rhymes and advertising make much use of these devices, which appeal to our fascination with echoes. Recall the thrill you felt when you first discovered an echo—had you hollered across a canyon or shouted into a cave or spoken loudly in an empty cathedral sanctuary or auditorium? Remember how weird but satisfying it was just to hear your own voice come back to you? Unexpected similarities are always thrilling, even in the sounds of the words we use.

Alliteration and assonance are comforting. From our earliest days we use them in call-and-response rituals in schools and religious services. And, of course, the poems within our hymns and prayers also use them. As you read and reread these lines from the Sermon on the Mount (Matthew 5), consider how the recurrent "r"s and the word *blessed* affect you.

> Blessed are the poor in spirit, for theirs is the kingdom of heaven.
> Blessed are those who mourn, for they will be comforted.
> Blessed are the meek, for they will inherit the earth.
> Blessed are those who hunger and thirst for righteousness, for they will be filled.
> Blessed are the merciful, for they will be shown mercy.
> Blessed are the pure in heart, for they will see God.
> Blessed are the peacemakers, for they will be called sons of God.
> Blessed are those who are persecuted because of righteousness, for theirs is the kingdom of heaven.

Or reflect on how you feel as you experience William Blake's repeated consonant and vowel sounds in *The Divine Image*:

> To Mercy, Pity, Peace, and Love
> All pray in their distress;
> And to these virtues of delight
> Return their thankfulness.
>
> For Mercy, Pity, Peace, and Love
> Is God, our father dear,
> And Mercy, Pity, Peace, and Love
> Is Man, his child and care.
>
> For Mercy has a human heart,
> Pity a human face,
> And Love, the human form divine,
> And Peace, the human dress.

Then every man, of every clime,
    That prays in his distress,
Prays to the human form divine,
    Love, Mercy, Pity, Peace.

And all must love the human form,
    In heathen, turk, or jew;
Where Mercy, Love, & Pity dwell
    There God is dwelling, too.

Alliteration and assonance encourage us to slow down or speed up purposefully, to quiet our racing thoughts and pay attention to what we say and how we say it. Words are sacred ("In the beginning was the Word, and the Word was with God, and the Word was God . . . ," John II). Buddhist teaching recommends that we strive to be mindful so that all of our senses are heightened and help us to act and speak appropriately, so that our speech is "right"—in other words, beneficial and not harmful to others! The Moon Lamp Sutra expresses the lesson in this way:

Whatever one sees to be another's mistake,
Do not declare it as a mistake—
You will receive the result
Of whatever actions you take.

Exercise: Appropriate Speech

Sit quietly for several minutes as you would most naturally. When you feel calm and centered and ready, open your journal and write down recent examples when you spoke inappropriately. Perhaps you spoke angrily to a bewildered friend before hanging up on him. Maybe you repeatedly interrupted your partner, hurting her feelings because you made her feel that you weren't listening to her. Perhaps you sent your child off to school with harsh words because his essay on history was late. Write down, as well as you can remember them, your exact words.

Next, rewrite them and strive to transform inappropriate speech into appropriate words. If you wish, use your appropriate words to write a poem. Look it over when you've finished your first draft, paying attention to how you repeated consonant and vowel sounds within each of your lines. How do they make what you have to say more effective?

Alliteration occurs when the poet creates similar sounds in the consonants of words that are placed in close proximity to one another. Celtic poetry is heavily alliterative, as is our Old English masterpiece *Beowulf.* These lines, translated by Nobel laureate Seamus Heaney, give us the sense and feel of the epic poem: "The fortunes of war favored Hrothgar./Friends and kinsmen flocked to his ranks,/ young followers, a force that grew . . ." The repeated *f* sounds in each line keep readers focused. They also make the lines more emphatic than they would be if the device were not present.

Exercise: Double Consonants, or An Exercise in Dexterity
In your journal, write half a dozen lines of poetry. Go back and balance each line with an *r* in the first half, and an *r* in the second half. This is an exercise in dexterity, in working with our Beowulf balance! For example, I might begin this exercise with the line, "I ran into so many walls, ruined was my nose!"

My translation of a poem by Rainer Marie Rilke may help inspire you in the exercise above.

Buddha in Glory

Moment of moments, core of cores,
Almond all-encased, growing sweet—
this cosmos, to the most remote stars
and far beyond them, is your lotus flesh and fruit.
Now nothing clings, now nothing holds you back;
your vastness reaches into endless space,
where the rich, prosperous fluids rise and flow.
Shining in your infinite peace,
billions of stars go spinning through the night,
blazing and flaming above your head.
In you is the presence-awareness that
will be, when all the stars go out.

Here is a classic, tongue-twisting example of alliteration
from childhood:

Peter Piper picked a peck
Of pickled peppers.
If Peter Piper picked a peck
Of pickled peppers,
How many pickled peppers
Did Peter Piper pick?*

More subtle yet equally memorable is Anne Stevenson's
Carol of the Birds. Note the effect of the echoing *s* sounds in the
following tercet (or three lines):

---

*Anyone who flawlessly recites this poem in under twenty seconds deserves
a special reward.

Plovers that stoop to sanctify the land
And scoop small, roundy mangers in the sand,
Swaddle a saviour each in a speckled shell.

In these and many other examples, sound effectively evokes feeling, clarifying the poet's intention.

The drawback to alliteration is this: it is seductively easy to write. Many inept poems (doggerel) are dominated by alliteration gone berserk. The consequence for the reader (and poet) can be the same as losing the reins on a galloping horse or the brakes in your car. Using poems containing alliteration run amok will produce the opposite effect to the one intended. Rather than achieving appropriate pacing and mindfulness, the reader races through the poem or prayer, mouthing the words but failing to connect with their meaning. This is the fruitless practice of a sleepwalker. But when alliteration is matched to emotion and intention, it can be a rich resource of connection and devotion.

Exercise: Identifying Alliteration
Identify and discuss with a friend the alliteration in the following poem.

Valley Candle

My candle burned alone in an immense valley.
Beams of the huge night converged upon it,
Until the wind blew.
Then beams of the huge night
Converged upon its image,
Until the wind blew.
    (Wallace Stevens)

Exercise: Alliteration in Your Own Poem
Identify alliteration in a poem or fragment of your own.

Exercise: Consonant-Crazy
Make up a list of twenty-five words containing the consonants *B, P,* and *D.* Use these twenty-five words to write a poem.

Assonance occurs when the poet creates similar sounds in vowels of words in close proximity to one another. A deft instance can perfect a single line, as in this example from Emily Grosholz's poem, *The Abacus of Years:*

> We miss the lavish habits of repose.

The elegant *a* sounds feel good on the tongue and echo in the ear. Note, too, the alliterative *s*'s, reminding us that combining devices such as assonance and alliteration increases the odds that a poem will work. Consider this excerpt from A. A. Milne about a bear:

> I'd have a fur muffle-ruff to cover my jaws,
> And brown fur mittens on my big brown paws.
> With a big brown furry-down up to my head,
> I'd sleep all the winter in a big fur bed.

Those repetitions of the drumbeat *b*'s combine perfectly with the surging vowel sounds.

Like alliteration, assonance works its magic everywhere in the utterances that carry the intentions of spiritual practice out into the world. If alliteration mainly aids the pacing and emphasis of practice, then assonance creates a vessel in which emotion concentrates and wells up. Without even being aware of it, we feel a heart-ripening through assonance. Read aloud Christina Rossetti's poem *A Better Resurrection* and feel the plush, warm blanket sensations created by her luscious, repetitive vowel sounds.

I have no wit, no words, no tears;
My heart within me like a stone
Is numb'd too much for hopes or fears;
Look right, look left, I dwell alone;
I lift mine eyes, but dimm'd with grief
No everlasting hills I see;
My life is in the falling leaf:
O Jesus, quicken me.

My life is like a faded leaf,
My harvest dwindled to a husk:
Truly my life is void and brief
And tedious in the barren dusk;
My life is like a frozen thing,
No bud nor greenness can I see:
Yet rise it shall—the sap of Spring;
O Jesus, rise in me.

My life is like a broken bowl,
A broken bowl that cannot hold
One drop of water for my soul
Or cordial in the searching cold;
Cast in the fire the perish'd thing;
Melt and remould it, till it be
A royal cup for Him, my King:
O Jesus, drink of me.

Exercise: Identifying Assonance

Identify and discuss assonance in the following poem by John Milton:

On Shakespeare

What needs my Shakespeare for his honored bones,
The labor of an age in piled stones,
Or that his hallowed relics should be hid
Under a starry-pointing pyramid?
Dear son of memory, great heir of fame,
What needest thou such weak witness of thy name?
Thou in our wonder and astonishment
Hast built thyself a livelong monument.
For whilst to the shame of slow-endeavoring art,
Thy easy numbers flow, and that each heart
Hath from the leaves of thy unvalued book,
Those Delphic lines with deep impression took,
Then thou our fancy of itself bereaving,
Dost make us marble with too much conceiving;
And so sepulchered in such pomp dost lie,
That kings for such a tomb would wish to die.

Exercise: Assonance in Your Own Poems

Identify and share with friends assonance in a poem or fragment of your own.

Collaborative Exercise: Group Assonance

Invite a friend to tea and do this exercise together. Limit yourselves to three vowels. In twenty lines, see how many times you can use those vowels. Try again, substituting other vowels.

6

Rhyme and Meter

To varying degrees, examples of metaphor, simile, asso-nance, and alliteration may be found in any formal or free-verse poem. But what makes a formal poem different from a free-verse poem?

A formal poem often employs a recognizable rhyme scheme and features lines written in a particular meter.

Words or syllables that sound alike create a rhyme, as in this four-line stanza from Omar Khayyam's *The Rubaiyat*, a poem composed of sixty-four similar stanzas:

> In life devote yourself to joy and love
> Behold the beauty of the peaceful dove
> Those who live, in the end must all perish
> Live as if you are already in heavens above.

Love, *dove*, and *above* combine to create rhymes at the end of lines, while *joy*, *beauty*, and *already* create interior rhymes, or rhymes inside lines. Another example of interior rhyming occurs within these lines from *God's Grandeur* by the nine-teenth-century Jesuit priest Gerard Manley Hopkins:

And all is seared with trade; bleared, smeared with toil;
And wears man's smudge and shares man's smell:

In these lines, *seared, bleared*, and *smeared* rhyme in the first, while *wears* and *shares* rhyme in the second.

We tend to think of rhymes coming at the end of lines in a poem, but in fact a rhyme may fall anywhere in the line. We have already considered alliteration and assonance, which in fact create certain types of rhyme. The two other most common rhymes are full rhyme and slant (or, almost exact but not quite) rhyme. *Time/sublime* and *rock/flock* are examples of full rhyme, while *set/heat* and *son/down* are examples of slant rhyme. Rhyme is memorable, and can be fun, but as we have already acknowledged, it can also be tedious. Before writing, when poetry was purely an aural art, rhyme (and meter, too) made memorization easier for spiritual practitioners, teachers, and entertainers who told the stories that preserved and celebrated their people's cultural history.

The anonymous Celtic poem that follows surfaces out of the collective-unconscious mind of a nation rich in rain, rivers, and lakes, and reflects the preoccupation of a seafaring culture with death by water. Notice how the insistent end rhymes of the first three lines of each stanza contribute to creating the poem's somber tone, while the end rhyme of the fourth line rhyming with the end line of the stanza following it heightens one's sense of finality. The effect reminds me of the tolling of church bells.

How curious the light behaves
Reflecting off the dancing waves.
Oh how my very being craves
A view from down below.

Suspended in my watery lair,
I would not need to gasp for air,
For I'm no longer human there
Beneath the icy flow.

It's peaceful there, but I have found
I still can hear the distant sound
Of voices of the souls who drowned
And left loved ones to mourn.

The lonely wails transmit the pain
Of those who just could not remain
So journeyed to the unknown plane
Of dead souls and unborn.

But in this world there still exist
Survivors who will always miss
The passion of their lovers' kiss
That warmed them night and day.

Though here above the vast, cold sea,
My heart is without tragedy,
For I have someone dear to me
Who hasn't passed away.

Never let that be untrue,
For I could not bear thoughts of you
Trapped underneath the ocean blue
Deprived of your last breath.

No harm to you would I condone,
For I'd be left here on my own
To face this tragic world alone,
A fate far worse than death.

Exercise: Identifying Rhyme

Choose two poems you really enjoy, and with the help of friends, if you like, identify all of the rhymes in them you can find. Discuss what the poem might look and sound like without them.

Exercise: Dissecting Rhyme

Select a brief rhymed poem you enjoy, and describe in your journal the way rhyme contributes to the poem.

Collaborative Exercise: Round-Rhyming

Sit in a circle with two other writer friends and practitioners. Choose someone who will begin. That person should write a line on a piece of paper, then pass it to the person on her left; that person should write a second line, making sure to create an end rhyme with the last word of the line written by the person who went first. Continue around the circle at least four times. Stop and share what you've got.

In a variation of this exercise, the people taking the third, fifth, and seventh lines could take turns to create end rhymes with the last word of the line written by the person who wrote two turns before them. Another variation? Pass the paper around to the right instead of the left. You can come up with your own variations, too, and all of them can be great fun.

· · ·

Meter is the mechanics of organizing stressed and unstressed syllables in each line. Since Chaucer's time (the fourteenth century), the most popular meter in English has been iambic. An iamb is an unstressed syllable followed by a stressed syllable, as in _desire_. The underlined portion of the word is the stressed syllable. The word _desire_ is in fact an iambic foot. We call a line consisting of five iambic feet iambic pentameter. Here is an example from a popular birthday song:

> We'll <u>have</u> some <u>cake</u> and <u>sand</u>wiches and <u>lots</u>
> Of <u>ice</u> cream, <u>too</u>. We'll <u>sing</u> and <u>play</u> the <u>day</u>
> A<u>way</u>—there's <u>one</u> more <u>thing</u> we're <u>go</u>ing to <u>do</u> . . .

The stressed syllables are underlined. There are five stresses in each line.

There is no rule against including any number of feet in a line of formal poetry—by "formal" we mean poetry that is composed in a distinct, identifiable meter. The standard French poetry line, for example, is hexameter (six stressed syllables to a line). But most formal poems in English seldom exceed five feet (_Note_: two-foot lines are called dimeter, three-foot lines are called trimeter; four-foot lines are called tetrameter).

Here is a poem by the metaphysical master John Donne.

Hymn to God, My God, in My Sickness

Since I am coming to that holy room,
  Where, with thy choir of saints for evermore,
I shall be made thy music; as I come
  I tune the instrument here at the door,
  And what I must do then, think here before.

Whilst my physicians by their love are grown
    Cosmographers, and I their map, who lie
Flat on this bed, that by them may be shown
    That this is my south-west discovery
    Per fretum febris, by these straits to die,

I joy, that in these straits, I see my west;
    For, though their currents yield return to none,
What shall my west hurt me? As west and east
    In all flat maps (and I am one) are one,
    So death doth touch the resurrection.

Is the Pacific Sea my home? Or are
    The eastern riches? Is Jerusalem?
Anyan, and Magellan, and Gibralter,
    All straits, and none but straits, are ways to them,
    Whether where Japhet dwelt, or Cham, or Shem.

We think that Paradise and Calvary,
    Christ's Cross, and Adam's tree, stood in one place;
Look Lord, and find both Adams met in me;
    As the first Adam's sweat surrounds my face,
    May the last Adam's blood my soul embrace.

So, in his purple wrapped receive me Lord,
    By these his thorns give me his other crown;
And as to others' souls I preached thy word,
    Be this my text, my sermon to mine own,
    "Therefore that he may raise the Lord throws down."

This beautiful poem of end-rhymed, five-line stanzas was composed in flawless iambic pentameter on the poet's death-bed in March 1631. In it, Donne sees his death by fever as a gateway to eternity—a new world. The Latin phrase *per fretum febris* literally translates to "by the heart, and strait, of fever."

The iamb is our most popular unit (foot) in English poetry, but the trochee, its opposite, is also popular. The word _sup_er represents a trochaic foot in which a stressed syllable is followed by an unstressed syllable. _O_ver _hills_ and _vales_ and _squishy snails_ we _go_ on is an example of a trochaic hexameter (six stresses) line. Once again, the stressed syllables are under-lined. Unlike the iambic foot, the stressed syllable precedes the unstressed syllable rather than following it. Elizabeth Barrett Browning offers an excellent example of trochaic feet and lines in action.

The Best Thing in the World

What's the best thing in the world?
June-rose, by May-dew impearled;
Sweet south-wind, that means no rain;
Truth, not cruel to a friend;
Pleasure, not in haste to end;
Beauty, not self-decked and curled
Till its pride is over-plain;
Light, that never makes you wink;
Memory, that gives no pain;
Love, when, so, you're loved again.
What's the best thing in the world?
—Something out of it, I think.

Two other feet, anapest and dactyl, are also fairly common in formal poems in English.

The anapestic foot consists of two unstressed syllables followed by a stressed syllable. Here are examples: *in the <u>know</u>*, *up a <u>creek</u>*. The poet Joyce Kilmer, who died in battle in World War I and is buried in France, was fond of anapests. Here is his poem *Thanksgiving*, dedicated to John Bunker.

> The roar of the world is in my ears.
> Thank God for the roar of the world!
> Thank God for the mighty tide of fears
> Against me always hurled!
> Thank God for the bitter and ceaseless strife,
> And the sting of His chastening rod!
> Thank God for the stress and the pain of life,
> And Oh, thank God for God!

Anapests are essential to the movement and tone of this poem. They include *of the world* in line one, *for the roar* and *of the world* in line two.

Exercise: Spotting Anapests
Identify the anapests in the remaining six lines of Kilmer's *Thanksgiving*.

The dactylic foot consists of a stressed syllable followed by two unstressed syllables. <u>Ri</u>pening is one example; <u>sick</u>ening is another. The dactylic foot is more emphatic than the anapestic foot. If we compare the two to running waters, we might say that the dactyl is white water for advanced kayakers or rafters, while an anapestic foot is more like the white water that is more suitable for river novices. The first line of Henry Wadsworth Longfellow's venerable *Evangeline* contains six feet; the first five are dactyls:

> <u>This</u> is the/<u>for</u>est prim-/<u>ev</u>al. The / <u>mur</u>muring / <u>pines</u>
> and the / <u>hem</u>locks,

Can you identify the sixth foot in this line? We met it earlier in this chapter.

Of course, a famous poem in dactylic feet is Alfred, Lord Tennyson's *The Charge of the Light Brigade*. Here is a portion:

> Half a league, half a league,
> Half a league onward,
> All in the valley of Death
> Rode the six hundred.
> "Forward the Light Brigade!
> Charge for the guns!" he said.
> Into the valley of Death
> Rode the six hundred.
>
> "Forward, the Light Brigade!"
> Was there a man dismay'd?
> Not tho' the soldier knew
> Some one had blunder'd.
> Theirs not to make reply,
> Theirs not to reason why,
> Theirs but to do and die.
> Into the valley of Death
> Rode the six hundred.

Exercise: Identifying Dactyls

Pick any two of the stanzas in Tennyson's poem and underline all of the dactyls you can find. Write a few stanzas of your own using as many dactyls as seem appropriate.

On occasion, we may use, and discover in the formal poems of others, a spondee or a pyrrhic. These are two feet that may be substituted for one of the four major feet above.

A spondee is a foot consisting of two stressed syllables, as in _shipwreck_ or _big boy_. These lines from Tennyson's poem _Ulysses_ contain spondaic feet:

> Well-loved of me, discerning to fulfill
> This labor, by small prudence to make mild

The spondees are _Well-loved_, _This la——_, and _make mild_.

A pyrrhic is a foot consisting of two unstressed syllables, as in _in the_. Again, here is an example from Tennyson and his poem, _In Memorium:_

> When the blood creeps and the nerves prick
> And tingle; and the heart is sick,

The pyrrhic feet are _When the_ and _and the_ in line one, and _——le and_ in line two. The first line is notable for the fact that it consists entirely of pyrrhic and spondaic feet. The spondees are _blood creeps_ and _nerves prick_.

Spondaic and pyrrhic feet are used as substitutes within an established metrical pattern, most frequently anapestic meter. Tennyson made liberal use of both in his poetry.

Meter and rhyme trigger the brain in appealing to the ear and to memory. It's generally easier to remember a poem in rhyme and meter than a free-verse poem with no regular pattern. Think of any number of advertising slogans and jingles. Pay attention to these shadow forms of poetry all around you. Examples are everywhere.

For instance, I discovered an amusing, effective example along a stretch of Interstate 5 in California. About ninety miles south of Sacramento, I noticed a billboard at the edge of a sprawling orange grove. The sign featured two lines: IT'S EAST AND WEST!/IT'S ALL AROUND! Two miles farther on a second sign appeared with the lines IN THE MIDDLE/CROW CREEK IS FOUND. Two miles after that, a third sign appeared: IT CAN ALL BE YOURS/HOW DOES THAT SOUND?

These billboards romanced properties listed by Shane P. Donlon, ranch real-estate broker extraordinaire. In a twenty-mile stretch, I spotted ten of his billboards. Each one featured a couplet. Usually, two or three billboards were designed to be read in sequence. This is a wonderful way to capture a motorist's attention as she speeds along the highway! It doesn't matter that the couplets are doggerel, a decidedly low-octane grade of verse. What is important is that we acknowledge that there is something innately pleasing about words that sound alike, and lines that follow a recognizable pattern, a measure.

Nowhere is this pleasure born of potent words and rhythm more present than in spiritual practice. The use of rhyme and meter in advertising has a finite goal; it's employed to bring about a quick fix—a sale. But rhyme, meter, and rhythm in spiritual practice takes aim at no end. Rather, it calms and focuses the practitioner, making ever-evolving progress and change possible. In this way, poetry tunes a practitioner to the proper frequency, the one that leads to spiritual breakthrough.

Exercise: Writing Anapests and Dactyls

Write ten lines of anapestic verse and ten lines of dactylic verse. You should be able to hear and see that anapests create an almost mad-dash pace, a headlong rush, while dactyls seem to be more emphatic, with more distinctive stops along the way. For inspiration, read and reread this wonderful, heartbreaking poem about getting old and saying goodbye to passion by George Gordon, Lord Byron. The Canadian poet-songwriter Leonard Cohen beautifully set this poem to music on his 2004 album *Dear Heather*. Joan Baez also recorded it, and the poem is important in Ray Bradbury's *The Martian Chronicles*. Incredibly, the physically and spiritually exhausted Byron wrote this poem and included it in a letter to Thomas Moore at the age of twenty-nine. Every line except two and eight begins with an anapestic foot; lines one and nine end with dactylic feet; line twelve consists of two anapests.

So We'll Go No More A-Roving

So, we'll go no more a-roving
   So late into the night,
Though the heart be still as loving,
   And the moon be still as bright.

For the sword outwears its sheath,
   And the soul wears out the breast,
And the heart must pause to breathe,
   And love itself have rest.

Though the night was made for loving,
   And the day returns too soon,
Yet we'll go no more a-roving
   By the light of the moon.

Collaborative Exercise: Ganging Up on Meter

This is an excellent activity for a small party. With a group of friends, select three poems written in recognizable meters from any source. Scan the poems, identifying the metrical feet each poem employs. Later on (to have fun), substitute different metrical feet of your own composition in the poems and see what happens to the original. This exercise may make you laugh. You may find you've created an interesting alternative to the original poem. You may even discover a poetry bridge of your own devising that fits perfectly into your spiritual practice and enhances it. For instance, notice how this variation of Byron's stanza shed new light for me.

> Go no more a-roving, you,
> Alone, without a light.
> Shipwrecked in a liar's cove,
> Past prayer, forever night!

7

Stanza

We organize our words, figures of speech, meters, and rhythms into lines, and our lines into stanzas, the most basic form a poem can take. Some successful poems consist of a single stanza, and so it seems an inviting place to start.

"A stanza is the verse equivalent of a paragraph." So wrote the Pulitzer Prize–winning poet Karl Shapiro and coauthor Robert Beum in *A Prosody Handbook* (1965). Stanzas are islands in a storm of thought. Or we may think of them as liturgical units of devotion, or steps we take up the ladder of spiritual practice. A stanza is any line or group of lines in a poem set off from other groupings by an extra line of space. Like paragraphs, stanzas provide a frame within the larger frame of the poem itself for shaping our thoughts and stylistically and thematically controlling their progression. Each stanza guides our reading and interpretation much as signal lights modulate our driving and often manipulate the directions we choose to follow.

Stanzas allow the writer to make logical transitions, to advance plot, change course, build a case, intensify a song. Stanzas allow the reader to pace herself, even imagine participating in the making of the poem. Stanzas assist both in making sense of what is going on.

A stanza can be one line or limitless lines (though a stanza like the latter might drive a reader crazy). Here is a poem by Ginger Andrews, a prizewinning poet, professional house-cleaner, and Sunday school teacher from Coos Bay, Oregon. This poem has served my own spiritual practice well, especially when I meditate on humility.

What the Cleaning Lady Knows

Cleanliness is not and never has been next to godliness.

White carpets are hell.

You can get by without Comet, Spic and Span or lemon oil,
　　But Windex is mandatory.

Ammonia can cause pneumonia.

People who pay to have clean houses cleaned are lonely.

Children whose parents work full-time will fall in love with
　　you.

Rich people splatter diarrhea
On the inside rim of their toilet seats, just like the rest of us.

Cleaning rags should always be washed separately with
　　bleach.

Cash is better than checks.

This gritty poem is written in one-line and two-line stanzas. Each free-verse stanza comes as a deceptively simple revelation, a wise comment about people who are financially well off and those who provide services for them. Each revelation by itself inspires a pause, a moment of contemplation in which the reader tests the validity of the poet's assertion. Inevitably, one thinks of moments in one's own life in which similar experiences and revelations have occurred. The point of the poem, of course, is that all people, on some fundamental, human level, are equal.

Once again, stanzas can include any number of lines. Apprenticing yourself to the long history of stanza creation, you are going to work a little with three of the most popular and basic stanza forms, the couplet, the tercet, and the quatrain.

Couplet

There is something so appealing about things in twos. God and supplicant, salt and pepper, fish and chips, Simon and Garfunkel, mother and father, teacher and student, bat and glove, surf and turf, sun and moon, you and I . . . our lists could go on forever.

Couplets have the beauty of brevity and basic balance. They often carry a quick jab, a quip, and can be delightful for poking fun at somber subjects. One of the world's great epic poems, Geoffrey Chaucer's *The Canterbury Tales*, tells in couplets the stories of a large group of mostly middle-class strangers on a religious pilgrimage. Consider, however, these more recent examples from an autobiographical satire, *Poems of the Presidents*, in which the anonymous authors chose to represent some of the lesser lights of the White House through couplets.

William Henry Harrison

I don't believe in overcoats.
My lungs are a couple of sunken boats.

Harrison, you may recall, refused to wear an overcoat on his extremely chilly inauguration day, caught a cold, and died a month later, having failed to serve a single healthy day in office.

The authors of these poems apparently thought his descendant, also elected president, deserved a couplet, too. Harrison the Younger obviously learned a very important lesson from his star-crossed kinsman.

Benjamin Harrison

My lungs are pink inside their moats.
I believe in overcoats.

A third president whose legacy seemed to embody the crispness of a couplet was the ill-fated Warren G. Harding, who, to the chagrin of grammarians everywhere, successfully ran on the campaign slogan A Return to Normalcy (the word he was after was *normality*). Harding's abbreviated term in office has become identified with excessive partying and administrative corruption.

Warren G. Harding

I looked like a President, all my friends said.
Then they found me in a Pullman car, dead!

Finally, from this sequence there is Gerald Ford, Richard Nixon's second vice president who rose to the top job when his boss resigned in 1974. Ford, perhaps unfairly, was often lampooned for his physical clumsiness and plodding performance.

I'm just a couplet man. I'm nothing else.
In twelve months time I'll stumble on your shelves.

Some of you think that's funny, but it's sad.
Those were the best two years I ever had.

Because I pardoned him, you think I'm bad.
Now I'm an elder statesman with a cad.

Of course, not all couplets are satirical or even funny. Dialogue rich in suggestion can be contained by the couplet, as in these lines from George Crabbe's *Peter Grimes.* Here a son, in violent disagreement with his father, dismisses God and the Bible.

"It is the word of life!" the father cried.
"This is the life itself," the boy replied.

As small as they are, couplets can be downright magisterial. For proof, consider John Donne's poem *The Computation,* which is a marvelous aid to the contemplation of mortality and impermanence.

For the first twenty years since yesterday
I scarce believed thou couldst be gone away;
For forty more I fed on favors past,
And forty on hopes that thou wouldst they might last.
Tears drowned one hundred, and sighs blew out two,
A thousand, I did neither think nor do,
Or not divide, all being one thought of you,
Or in a thousand more forgot that too.
Yet call not this long life, but think that I
Am, by being dead, immortal. Can ghosts die?

Exercise: Two by Two by Two . . .
Compose six couplets, making use of the end words provided.

> sense
> penance
>
> variation
> devastation
>
> breathe
> beneath
>
> east
> sweet
>
> mother
> another
>
> planet
> it

Here are a few examples of couplets I wrote to these end words.

> She discovered she couldn't make sense
> Of his hunger for penance.
>
> Lazy and lewd, he wrote out a variation
> About money, luck, love, and devastation.

Oh to be named for a sea-blue planet,
And linger at the bus stop as people repeat it.

Now give it a try and see what you come up with.

Exercise: Arbitrary Couplets

Take the excerpt below from *Deciding the Course My Education Should Take* by Clemens Starck and restructure it, writing the lines in your notebook in couplets. Compare the two versions. What did you learn about forming lines of poetry into couplets?

> Maybe I already know
> as much as I'm destined to know, for this lifetime,
> about small-engine repair.
> And also about plumbing.
> For that matter, I wouldn't mind
> drinking a beer
> to celebrate
> an end to plumbing, and an end to small-engine repair.

Is anything gained by reshaping this stanza into couplets? How does rhythm change? What about meaning? What is lost? How might you change the words if you want the poem to be written in successful couplets?

Exercise: Couplet Crazy

Fill a page in your journal with couplets of your own. Remember, you can praise the Supreme Being, invent dialogue, tell a story, celebrate a person, sell a product, or express your anger in a couplet. Once you have completed your page, go back to determine how many of your couplets can stand alone. How many can be put together to form a longer poem of couplets? When you have accomplished that much, the tercet awaits.

Tercet

Threesomes of any kind suggest greater social skills than are found in pairs. More compromise and planning inevitably govern groups larger than two. In his wonderful essay, "Baseball and the American Character," the late A. Bartlett Giamatti notes that the game is "built on multiples of three, nine players play nine innings, with three outs to a side, each out possibly composed of three strikes." Think of the complexities inherent in the relationships between dogs in a pack, between a married couple and an in-law, between three brothers or sisters, between a woman and two men who love her.

The lines of the tercet may rhyme consecutively (also called a triplet); they may make use of interlocking rhyme (also called terza rima); they may not rhyme at all (also called a tristich).

Here is a poem in tercets by Elise Paschen.

House Through Leaves

They raised the house through leaves
which flared and burned blood-red,
topaz, magenta, plum.

They raised the house. She was
a house where he would live
and pile the logs, the branches.

Around the house he staked
our earth before the sun
slipped down, although the leaves

shone through the night dark as
her hair which tumbled dusk-like
about her open face

by whose light he would labor.
He planted his fence, post
by post, before the leaves.

Before they fell. Before
the sap, the bud, the shoot.
They raised the house through leaves.

The tercets compel us forward as if we were climbing a tree,
hopping from branch to branch. Paschen makes superb use
of repetition, even echoing forms (the villanelle, the rondel)
that we will meet later on. The first and last lines of the poem
are identical. The third line and penultimate line are shadow
images of each other. The word *leaves* actually ends four of the
poem's fifteen lines. Combined with the subject, the nature of
creating a physical home, and home in an important psychic
sense, Paschen's insistent, repetitive rhythm and word choice
enhances the poem's air of mystery, even grandeur.

Exercise: End Words Await!
Compose three tercets that include the end words provided.

disease
cease
cheese

her
bumper
prayer

break
make
lake

Here are my attempts.

I'm sick of this disease!
Your picking and hacking must cease.
So must your diet of rank cheese.

The driver of the stalled car asked if I'd jump her.
I smiled, putting my foot on her bumper,
And said, of course, just let me finish my prayer.

"Some," you groan, "just never get a break."
"You're right," I say. "They're always on the make,
And end up floating face-down in a lake."

Now, you try.

When Christians think of tercets as spiritual practice, they think first of the Holy Trinity, in which God resides forever as three beings, the Father, the Son, and the Holy Spirit. Tercets are integral to the writing and sense of Dante's *The Divine Comedy* in which, in *The Inferno*, sinners are condemned to levels of Hell for sins such as envy, gluttony, anger, and lust, among others.

Percy Bysshe Shelley composed *Ode to the West Wind* to celebrate the power and inevitability of change, which would sweep through the world carried by the wind. He wrote the poem in tercets except for the concluding couplet in each of the poem's five sections, or cantos. Here is the fifth canto:

Make me thy lyre, even as the forest is:
What if my leaves are falling like its own?
The tumult of thy mighty harmonies

Will take from both a deep autumnal tone,
Sweet though in sadness. Be thou, Spirit fierce,
My spirit! Be thou me, impetuous one!

Drive my dead thoughts over the universe
Like wither'd leaves, to quicken a new birth;
And, by the incantation of this verse,

Scatter, as from an unextinguish'd hearth
Ashes and sparks, my words among mankind!
Be through my lips to unawaken'd earth

The trumpet of a prophecy! O Wind,
If Winter comes, can Spring be far behind?

Exercise: I Must Have...
Make a list of twelve things you could not possibly live without (you may include in your list names of people or animals if you wish). Make each of these twelve things the first word in four tercet stanzas. Complete the stanzas. When you are finished, you should have four tercets.

Collaborative Exercise: A Game of Catch

Play a game of tercet catch with a partner. Pair up. Decide who goes first and write a beginning line. The second person writes a line; go back to the first person, who writes the third line. Continue until you've come up with thirty lines, ten stanzas of three lines each. Do you have a poem? Are you on your way to one? Can you salvage lines for later use elsewhere? This exercise can produce interesting results if you try it with three people, too. Discuss how the poems you have just cocreated might work in spiritual practice.

Quatrain

A stanza consisting of four lines is called a quatrain. Universally, four is a comforting number. If *two* delivers comfort and brevity, *four* doubles your pleasure. Among children, a favorite game involves taking positions in a square divided into four sections and bouncing a ball into sections other than the one you occupy. The game continues until one hits a line with the ball, hits the ball out of the square, or misses the ball altogether.

American four-square was for decades a popular architectural home style. Storytellers and travelers once frequently referred to "the four corners of the globe." Foursomes regularly tee off at public and private golf courses around the world. Football stadiums, tennis courts, and basketball courts are laid out in rectangles, the close first cousin of the square. Each contains two goals, and plenty of organized room for observers and opposing teams. Handkerchiefs are cut in squares. So are brownies, sliced bread, CD boxes. It's true that *square* has a pejorative use implying a certain blockheadedness, a certain oafishness (as in the opposite of *cool*), but *square* also implies an undeniable rightness of stature and character. A square connotes security, comfort, a structure that is capable of protecting the home fires.

In poetry, the quatrain is the most popular stanza form in the English language. Its balance makes it so. This also informs the quatrain's appeal in spiritual practice, for it suits those segments involving meditation by creating appropriate space around the practitioner's effort. Couplet and tercet stanzas, in contrast, are swifter and more transitional.

Here is a poem by John Keats consisting of two quatrains. Note how the lines alternate between four and three stresses. The simple, effective rhyme scheme can be described as ABAB CDCD.

Sweet, Sweet Is the Greeting of Eyes

Sweet, sweet is the greeting of eyes,
And sweet is the voice in its greeting,
When adieus have grown old and goodbyes
Fade away where old time is retreating.

Warm the nerve of a welcoming hand,
And earnest a kiss on the brow,
When we meet over sea and o'er land
Where furrows are new to the plow.

Notice how in each quatrain the first two lines assert facts, while the last two lines of each stanza provide the conditions for the assertions to come to fruition. Often, meditation in its early stages works just this way! Neither the couplet, the tercet, nor any other stanza form achieves this balance so well.

Here is another poem in quatrains by Frederick Morgan.

1932

At Twelfth Street and Fifth Avenue
in front of the old Longchamps
one frigid winter morning, as
I watched for the bus to come,

I saw a dark unshaven man
whose skin was snowy pale
set up a stand at the corner. He
had bright red apples for sale

a nickel each, but no one stopped
to look; they walked on by.
He stood there coatless, shivering,
with a fever in his eye

until a small blonde shape appeared,
a child of three or four,
who came from nowhere I could see—
no one accompanied her.

She wore a blue wool coat, fur-trimmed
to warm her wrists and neck,
fur hat, thick gloves and leggings to block
the cold from every crack—

she ran straight to the tattered man,
hugged him around both knees,
tipped back her head and stared straight up:
I couldn't read her gaze.

And there they stood, she holding fast
as though she'd seized her own,
he making no move to escape
but smiling grimly down . . .

I never saw the end, nor learned
what it was those two might tell.
My bus pulled up, I climbed aboard—
and was on my way to school.

This succeeds at what poetry does so well—preserves and recreates a commonplace scene that resonates with mystery and significant feeling. Is the man the girl's father or a stranger? The poem's dramatic impact sways considerably from one extreme to another depending on our answer. Ambiguity is perfectly established in the series of balancing quatrains. The poem witnesses and testifies to the commonality of the human experience and spirit.

Exercise: End Words Included
Compose two quatrains to the end words provided.

> father
> door
> mother
> tore
>
> breeze
> torch
> ease
> march

Here are my attempts.

I wish I believed in a father
Who opened a cloud like a door,
And bowed to reconciled mother,
And mended the hearts he tore.

Your voice is a breeze,
Your hand is a torch,
Cooling with ease
And lighting the seeker's march.

Now, you try it.

Exercise: Twos Morph into Fours

From your journal, collect four of your couplets and attempt to arrange them into two quatrains. Next, try to reimagine and rearrange four of your triplets into three quatrains. Write two paragraphs explaining what this teaches you about progression of sequence, about pacing. Finally, attempt a new poem consisting of four quatrains.

Exercise: Reconstructing a Mentor's Lines

Poems can be conceived in any number of ways; they may assume any shape and form. Here is a poem by Colette Inez in the form of a letter. The speaker in the poem is a woman writing to a friend, a photographer who may or may not be the woman's lover. There is separation, perhaps on many issues, between the two, separation that the poem hopes to bridge. After thoroughly experiencing the poem on its own terms, rearrange it into quatrains. What is gained, or lost? You may also enjoy including this poem in your spiritual practice when you meditate on separation, loss, and letting go. Poems are valuable processes of investigation.

Red August Letter

Dear Friend:

The day you brought me geraniums,
my period came. That night I had a red dream,
red walls, lamps. You were a photographer
in a darkroom developing shots I couldn't
quite make out. I asked how you balanced
opposing needs. You shrugged and lifted
pictures out of a chemical bath.

In the photo you left of the party, who is
the feral-looking poet in the rumpled suit?
Woman-hater? Once I would have memorized his poems.
The rain goes on. I've read your note, its chaste,
familiar script on a monogrammed blue page. I write.
My paper laps up ink. Stamps curl. A vague
taste of stickum lingers in my mouth.

Slack hours. Do you ever imagine the atoms
of your watch pulsing in a fading light?
Take a stand, intones my clock from its orderly
frontier. I resolve to reconcile odds and ends,
to inspect, put things out of sight, receive
the house-god, give him loose-skinned oranges,
an offering for auspicious news.

Was it last spring, after we'd found the cardinal's
nest fastened to a branch of pine, we spoke of ways
to stave off birth? What I didn't say was that
my scrap of a child sometimes floats in the back
of my head like a sea-creature, open-mouthed
as if it were startled or in pain to learn its
name would not be called.

Why hadn't I known of the Zulu woman
who counted stars in her labor from a hole
in the ceiling of her hut? Would knowing it
have changed the fact I didn't have the spunk
to watch the tight bud open to a rose,
giving birth to a red dream, to alpha, a letter
in August, giving birth to fingerprints
in a spectrum of light?

Tonight Mars and Venus are aligned in the summer
sky. Come with your prints and films. All week
opulent sunsets have fallen on soaked roads.
Forecasters say nothing we haven't heard.
I want to hear your reflector dream, your daughter
dream, to be brought into communion with old ghosts.

Think about writing a letter to someone you know, or would
like to know, or to someone you knew, perhaps, in another
life. Selecting any form with which you feel comfortable, com-
pose the letter as a poem and share it with a friend, a prayer
group or writing group. If appropriate, send it to the person
you write to!

Collaborative Exercise: Building Poems by Fours
Alternate writing the lines of a quatrain with a partner. Next, alternate writing couplets within quatrains. Then alternate writing quatrains until you have three poems you would like to share with friends.

Three

Forms for Practice

8

Haiku:
Perfection of a Seed

Haiku is one of the most popular Asian forms to grace American poetry. The therapist and hymn writer Maureen Hicks has said that she often experiences haiku as spiritual practice. Traditionally referring to a season or other elements of the natural world, haiku is like a delicate focal point to the contemplative mind. There is no room in the haiku for busyness or a chattering mind. Several examples follow.

> Black cloudbank broken
> Scatters in the night . . . Now see
> Moon-lighted mountain!
>
> *(Basho)*

On the Death of His Child

> Dew evaporates
> And all our world is dew . . . so dear,
> So fresh, so fleeting.
>
> *(Issa)*

Haiku (for Paul Robeson)

your voice unwrapping
itself from the Congo
contagious as shrines.

(Sonia Sanchez)

The laden wagon runs
Rumbling and creaking down the road.
Three peonies tremble.

(Buson)

Take the round flat moon
Snap this twig for a handle.
What a pretty fan!

(Sokan)

The flowering bush
With only one bloom, the rest
Shut for the winter.

(Jane Mary Katherine McDowell)

In unending rain
The house-pent boy is fretting
With his brand-new kite.

(Shoha)

Senryu is a variation of haiku that features humor instead
of seasons and the natural world. The Basho translation below
is one example, and the haiku that follows is another.

Only one guy and
Only one fly trying to
Make the guest room do.
                    (Basho, trans. Cid Corman)

He did it—Mickey
Mantle in bike spokes. A boy
adds up his losses.

It seems that every generation of American poets produces at least some memorable poems in this supposedly simple, unadorned form. A well-written haiku is a beautiful vessel, like a seed (a vessel containing life itself). It's a tricky business, attaining the perfection of a seed. If wisdom is an essential component of haiku, then the form itself encourages the writer to traverse the precarious path toward emotional, spiritual breakthrough.

A legend has it that one day a pilgrim visited a grove of five sacred oak trees. Out of each tree grew seven limbs, and on all but the bottom two limbs of each tree perched a bird's nest. A farmer rested under the shade of the tree nearest the road, where a pilgrim joined him.

"How long," the pilgrim asked, "has each tree had seven limbs, and birds' nests on all but the lower two limbs?"

"Forever," the farmer replied. "Since before the question could even be conceived. Since the beginning, five-seven-five."

Haiku in Japanese literally means "beginning-verse." It is an excellent form for a writer in English to study and practice if one wishes to write in syllabics, which means counting the syllables, rather than the feet, in each line.

The haiku is made up of seventeen syllables. Lines one and three contain five syllables, while line two contains seven. Traditionally, haiku includes the name of a season, or a word or words that suggest a particular season, but in contemporary American haiku this requirement is often discarded.

Basho (1644–1694), a Zen Buddhist student in later life, is generally considered the great master of haiku. Buson (1715–1783) and Issa (1763–1827) are also widely celebrated as profound masters of the form.

As Basho and others who followed him knew, the spiritual journey is possible only if we learn how to pay attention to the smallest details, those facts we overlook so easily because we are in a hurry, too busy, too anxious to slow down, to watch and wait. This demanding process of mindfulness requires the patience of an earthworm, a snail. You strive to transport yourself into the thready veins of the apple blossom, the tiny bones of a bird's ear. Haiku asks us to slow down, to recognize and appreciate the minute details that make up and give substance to life itself. As Robert Frost once said, poetry is a way of remembering what it would impoverish us to forget. Haiku is an effective structure for mindfulness and memory.

Writers who include haiku in their writing and spiritual practice eventually notice significant breakthroughs in both. Working in miniature is an exacting practice. Every syllable counts; every syllable must be just right. Observation and accuracy are essential. Basho wrote, "Haiku is simply what is happening in this place at this moment." The profound poetry of total awareness and presence, haiku helps us discover the gold nugget in a seemingly played-out, barren hillside. It unlocks the great positive energy in modesty and honesty.

Exercise: Making Lists

Haiku requires that you use in your writing what you observe with all of your senses. In your notebooks, make a list of four smells you are aware of at this moment. Make a second list of three colors you see. Make a third list of five things you see out the window. Make a fourth list of four things you observe on the floor or ground. Make a fifth list of characteristics you observe in someone or several people near by.

From these lists, compose ten haiku. Finally, write three prose paragraphs describing the sensations you became aware of as you composed your haiku. Isn't it fascinating that your haiku says in three lines what your paragraphs say in—how many words?

Include your new haiku in your spiritual practice as you focus on simplicity, joy, balance, and harmony.

Exercise: Sacred Places

A haiku often contains an observation, a snapshot, of nature. Make a list of five places that are special, even sacred, for you. If you can, spend some quiet time in each of these places, or visit them in your mind, and compose three haiku at each one. Write a couple of paragraphs detailing your discoveries in this process. Share the poems and your revelations with your spiritual community.

Exercise: Spring Cleaning

Spend some time in your house, apartment, or dorm room. If you live with someone, ask her (or his) permission to examine the contents of her dresser or closet. Use only what you find there to create five haiku. What do they reveal about your roommate?

Exercise: Walking Poem

Take a walk through your neighborhood and concentrate on breathing deeply, evenly. Be open to observation. Come home and write six haiku using your observations. How accurate is the portrait of your neighborhood in the poems? Include them in your practice on wisdom and openness.

Tanka

Haiku actually began as part of another form called tanka. Here, courtesy of Lewis Turco, is an example of tanka:

> *Have you spoken aloud? Here,*
> *Where the swallows' crewel-work*
> *Sews the sky with mist?*
> You must cut the filament.
> You must be the lone spider.

In tanka, the first three lines follow the haiku pattern (though in our example Turco varies the pattern by using seven syllables in line 1). The last two lines of the tanka are traditionally composed of seven syllables each. Japanese poets would often pair up and write a tanka together. One poet would write the first three lines (the haiku), and the other poet would compose two closing lines to cap it. No form better illustrates poetry's communicative mechanism, its friendliness to dialogue.

Collaborative Exercise

Pair up with a friend and compose six tanka poems. Alternate positions, writing the first three lines, then the two lines that cap the poem. What does it tell you about different sensibilities and points of view? What does it teach about balance?

9

Sonnet:
Be Nimble, Be Quick

The sonnet is one of the most durable forms in poetry, and is periodically reviled and revived. The sonnet's brevity—fourteen lines—makes it attractive. It can present a complete argument with a conclusion, celebrate or lament love, tell a story, or comment on spiritual or worldly conditions. Sonnets can even recast other honored forms. In two very good examples, Sara Henderson Hay uses familiar fairy tales.

I Remember Mama

The trouble is, I never felt secure.
There we were, crammed into that wretched shoe,
Ragged and cold and miserably poor,
And Mama never knowing what to do.
Most of the time we lived on watery stew,
She couldn't even bake a loaf of bread,
And every night she'd thrash us black and blue
And send the sniveling lot of us to bed.

I used to lie awake for hours, and plan
The things I'd do, when I became a man ...
And this is why I lurk in darkened hallways,
And prowl dim streets and lonely parks, and always
Carry a knife, in case I meet another
Old woman who reminds me of my mother.

Juvenile Court

Deep in the oven, where the two had shoved her,
They found the Witch, burned to a crisp, of course.
And when the police had decently removed her,
They questioned the children, who showed no remorse.
"She threatened us," said Hansel, "with a kettle
Of boiling water, just because I threw
The cat into the well." Cried little Gretel,
"She fussed because I broke her broom in two,

And said she'd lock up Hansel in a cage
For drawing funny pictures on her fence ..."
Wherefore the court, considering their age,
And ruling that there seemed some evidence
The pair had acted under provocation,
Released them to their parents, on probation.

The sonnet is a perfect form for developing our apprenticeship in rhyme and meter, and for creating and discovering potent new material for spiritual reflection. The sonnet is so versatile! Many of Shakespeare's sonnets work well in meditations on yearning, love, reverence, and faith. Robinson Jeffers's sonnets work well in meditations on transformation and unity. The more we investigate, the more we'll discover sonnets that will enrich practice.

Mark Jarman, a poet who lives in Nashville, Tennessee, and

holds the Centennial Chair at Vanderbilt University, has written some of the best contemporary sonnets to explore spiritual themes. He writes that "the sonnet is a paradigmatic form of lyric poetry. Most short lyric poems between 10 and 20 lines have some structural similarity to the 14-line sonnet. On the page its four-square shape corresponds to the portrait and the box step, the classic American house architecture, the garden plot and the map. Its internal structure brings to mind the syllogism and the proof, the anecdote and the joke."

Some poets only grudgingly discover the beauty and significance of a good sonnet. The great William Carlos Williams, for instance, had no use for sonnets until he read some written by his contemporary, Merrill Moore. In a January 1938 letter to his publisher, James Laughlin, Williams explained his awakening.

> I have for years been stating that the sonnet is an outmoded form that can no longer be written. The sonnet, I see now, is not a form at all, but a state of mind. It is the extremely familiar dialogue upon which much writing is founded: a statement, then a rejoinder of a sort, perhaps a reply, perhaps a variant of the original—but a comeback of one sort or another . . . preserved the true sonnet, rescued it Perseus-like from its barren rock . . . . I never had the intelligence to realize that it wasn't the sonnet that was at fault but the bad artists who wrote in the form that were the calamity. The imagination rescues us all but how difficult to realize the simplest formulations until someone, some ONE, liberates us. Now sonnets can be written again.

I like Dr. Williams's vision of the sonnet as a comeback of sorts. Isn't that what we are always listening for, or trying to write, when we read or write a poem? Aren't we always trying to come back to something important we've lost or partially forgotten? We're hungry for a better answer than the one that may first have occurred to us. This searching is part of the motivation behind writing, creating, and spiritual practice. Williams's explanation is also a subtle example of mentoring and apprenticeship, for Merrill Moore mentored Williams in the virtues and possibilities of the sonnet.

In English, the sonnet is most often one of three types: the English (or Petrarchan) sonnet, the Italian sonnet, and the little-used Spenserian sonnet.

In rhyme and stanza, the English sonnet generally follows this pattern:

First quatrain
A
B
A
B

Second quatrain
C
D
C
D

Third quatrain
E
F
E
F

Final couplet
G
G

The early-sixteenth-century poet Thomas Wyatt is often credited with introducing the sonnet in English, both through his own sonnets and through translations of sonnets by Petrarch, an Italian poet of the fourteenth century. Here is an example, courtesy of Wyatt, of the English sonnet.

Sonnet 134

I find no peace, and all my war is done;
I fear and hope; I burn and freeze like ice;
I fly above the wind, yet can I not arise;
And nought I have, and all the world I seize on;

That looseth nor locketh holdeth me in prison
And holdeth me not, yet can I 'scape nowise;
Nor letteth me live nor die at my device
And yet of death it giveth none occasion

Withouten eyen, I see; and without tongue I plain;
I desire to perish, and yet I ask health;
I love another, and thus I hate myself;
I feed me in sorrow, and laugh in all my pain;

Likewise displeaseth me both death and life;
And my delight is causer of this strife.
   (Petrarch)

And here is another example by the form's greatest writer, William Shakespeare:

Sonnet 30

When to the sessions of sweet silent thought
I summon up remembrance of things past,
I sigh the lack of many a thing I sought,
And with old woes new wail my dear time's waste:
Then can I drown an eye, unused to flow,
For precious friends hid in death's dateless night,
And weep afresh love's long since cancell'd woe,
And moan the expense of many a vanish'd sight:
Then can I grieve at grievances foregone,
And heavily from woe to woe tell o'er
The sad account of fore-bemoaned moan,
Which I new pay as if not paid before.
But if the while I think on thee, dear friend,
All losses are restored and sorrows end.

In rhyme and stanza, the Italian sonnet generally follows this pattern:

Octave
First quatrain
A
B
B
A
Second quatrain
A
B
B
A

Volta

Sestet
First tercet
C
D
E
Second tercet
C
D
E

With a small variation in the closing tercet, here is an example of the Italian sonnet by John Milton.

XXIII. On His Deceased Wife

Methought I saw my late espoused saint
    Brought to me like Alcestis from the grave,
    Whom Jove's great son to her glad husband gave,
    Rescued from death by force though pale and faint.
Mine as whom washed from spot of child-bed taint,
    Purification in the old law did save,
    And such, as yet once more I trust to have
    Full sight of her in heaven without restraint,
Came vested all in white, pure as her mind:
    Her face was veiled, yet to my fancied sight,
    Love, sweetness, goodness, in her person shined
So clear, as in no face with more delight.
    But O as to embrace me she inclined
    I waked, she fled, and day brought back my night.

In rhyme and stanza, the Spenserian sonnet generally follows this pattern:

First quatrain
A
B
A
B

Second quatrain
B
C
B
C

Third quatrain
C
D
C
D

Couplet
E
E

This sonnet form is named after Edmund Spenser, the fifteenth-century author of *The Faerie Queene.* Here is a sonnet written by Spenser, number seven of a seven-part sequence titled *The Visions of Petrarch.* The poem is a marvelous piece for a meditation on attachment.

When I beheld this fickle trustless state
Of vain worlds glory, flitting to and fro,
And mortal men tossed by troublous fate
In restless seas of wretchedness and woe,
I wish I might this weary life forgo,
And shortly turn unto my happy rest,
Where my free spirit might not any moe
Be vext with sights, that do her peace molest.
And ye fair Lady, in whose bounteous breast
All heavenly grace and virtue shrined is,
When ye these rythmes do read, and vew the rest,
Loath this base world, and think of heaven's bliss:
And though ye be the fairest of God's creatures,
Yet think, that death shall spoil your goodly features.

Exercise: Writing to the End Words

In your notebook, copy the following words down the right-hand margin. Skip a line after the fourth, eighth, and twelfth lines.

cold
rest
sold
Everest

ever
lost
summer
cost

tomorrow
break
follow
awake

strong
long

Consider the words. Beginning at the left-hand margin, write lines to each end word. Don't worry about making sense from line to line. Let the end words inspire you. In fifteen or twenty minutes, you should be able to write fourteen lines. Congratulations! You have just accomplished your first draft of a sonnet.

Remind yourself, as Mark Jarman does in the commentary that follows, that forms can be altered, mixed and matched, according to your intention. No form is intended to be a tightly laced corset, forcing the breath out of the wearer. These forms actually provide you with the basis for endless experimentations and boundless freedom.

Here is a sonnet exercise developed by Mark Jarman.

Exercise: Mix and Match: The Variable Sonnet

"When Petrarch wrote in the Italian form of the sonnet, he spent the first eight lines, or octave, comparing some aspect of his beloved Laura with a natural phenomenon, for example, her face with the sun, and regretting that it did not shine on him; he filled the last six lines, or sestet, with some resolution of how he was to deal with this torment, e.g. by seeking obscurity or hoping for a heavenly reward.

"Shakespeare, on the other hand, followed the English form by, for example, lining up three parallel metaphors for the nature of his misery or happiness, in each of the three quatrains; in the final couplet, he tied them up, sometimes too neatly, with a summary of his feeling or an appeal to the maker of his misery or happiness. And yet there are times when Shakespeare actually follows the organization of an Italian sonnet, with a turn in his argument (the volta) after line eight, and a final six lines of resolution. And if you look into many of Petrarch's sonnets, you will see each octave is divided into two quatrains, each sestet into two tercets, not unlike the four-part structure of the English sonnet.

The fact is each of the forms can be made to behave like its counterpart. They can mix and match their rhyme schemes, too. James Wright's *Saint Judas* is an excellent example that combines elements of both the English and Italian sonnet."

When I went out to kill myself, I caught
A pack of hoodlums beating up a man.
Running to spare his suffering, I forgot
My name, my number, how my day began,
How soldiers milled around the garden stone
And sang amusing songs; how all that day
Their javelins measured crowds; how I alone
Bargained the proper coins and slipped away.

Banished from Heaven, I found this victim beaten,
Stripped, kneed, and left to cry. Dropping my rope
Aside, I ran, ignored the uniforms:

Then I remembered bread my flesh had eaten,
The kiss that ate my flesh. Flayed without hope,
I held the man for nothing in my arms.

"The octave rhymes like an English sonnet's first two quatrains. The sestet, however, follows the rhyme scheme and the structure of the Italian sestet; notice how it breaks into two tercets. The other poetic form Wright's sonnet recalls is the dramatic monologue; the other narrative mode it recalls is the anecdote. There is hardly a subject or rhetorical form the sonnet cannot accommodate. When part of a sequence, it can even unfold like a novel, as in George Meredith's *Modern Love*, which is made up, incidentally, of fifty 16-line sonnets. Here is number one:"

By this he knew she wept with waking eyes:
That, at his hand's light quiver by her head,
The strange low sobs that shook their common bed
Were called into her with a sharp surprise,
And strangely mute, like little gasping snakes,
Dreadfully venomous to him. She lay
Stone-still, and the long darkness flowed away
With muffled pulses. Then, as midnight makes
Her giant heart of Memory and Tears
Drink the pale drug of silence, and so beat
Sleep's heavy measure, they from head to feet
Were moveless, looking through their dead black years,
By vain regret scrawled over the blank wall.
Like sculptured effigies they might be seen
Upon their marriage-tomb, the sword between;
Each wishing for the sword that severs all.

"The form can do almost anything. Try a version like Wright's in which you begin with two quatrains in the English style, and end with an Italian sestet. You may also wish to tell a brief story. If you can't invent a persona, like the character Judas who speaks Wright's poem, take a look at a poem like *Reuben Bright* by Edwin Arlington Robinson. There, Robinson invents a character and tells his tragic tale. If narrative isn't for you, then return to the rhetorical structure of the Italian or English sonnet. Make an argument to the effect that if A occurs, then B is sure to follow, or if A, B, and C are true, then what about D? The possibilities are endless, like the internal workings of the atom."

Exercise: Fairy Tales

Take a favorite fairy tale or story from your childhood and recast it as a sonnet. Share your sonnet with your writing group during a special Fairy Tale Hour. Remember that writing poetry and listening to poetry ought to be fun! Here is an example of a Spenserian sonnet by the Texas poet Scott Wiggerman written for an exercise at the Taos Writers' Conference in 2004:

Hard Love in New Orleans

My parents were always over the top,
so it wasn't enough that they threw me out.
Before I could recover from that wallop
of rejection, a double-fisted knock-out,
they made the most of their God-given clout:
my photograph emblazoned over an obituary
in the Picayune, and—to seal all doubt—

a gravestone with dates for the parish to see.
If I could not adhere to their rules or be
the Christian girl they had reared,
then they clearly wanted no part of me.
I was dead, the daughter who disappeared.
For thirty hard years I've lived my demise.
The crime? Being gay, without compromise.

Exercise: Setting Up Your Own End-Word Exercise

Select your own end words that correspond to the rhyme scheme in the poem above. Copy those words in your workbook down the right-hand margin. Then, as you did in the first exercise on the sonnet, write lines culminating in each end word. This will constitute your first draft of a Spenserian sonnet.

Collaborative Exercise: Sonnet Slumber Party

With a partner, compose alternating lines for three sonnets (Elizabethan, Italian, and Spenserian). You may also do this exercise with more than one partner. Keep in mind that any time we work with others we are acting out two roles: mentor and apprentice.

Finally, here is a wonderful sonnet by Kate Light—about writing sonnets!

How Sonnets Are Like Bungee Jumping

It's the calculated danger—leap! The form will hold
you—will be as arms around you—ropes—
so when you say: *If I could be so bold . . .*
it says, *Okay, then, go! Spew out in hopes!*

There's safety in measure—like a mother
back at the shore, singing: *Swim out, and wave!*
Or (my Alexander teacher would say) a big brother
in your spine: *He's here; be brave.*
What's scary for someone's nothing for
another; to say, *Love;* to say, *I love,*
may be frightening as all get-out. And for
the very lucky, a poem can be a glove
that fits the hand that is your soul.
Oh, we jump in pieces; and some of us land whole.

10

Villanelle:
The Power of Echo

The villanelle is the most popular French form of modest length that made its way into English (we will consider the longer French form, the sestina, in our next chapter). A villanelle consists of nineteen lines and is usually composed in a pattern of five tercets and a closing quatrain. Like its shorter cousins the rondeau and rondel, the villanelle makes use of only two rhymes.

It also makes use of elaborate, almost visceral patterning. As a child, did you ever connect two tin cans with a piece of string, then talk with a friend through them? The effect produced by those crude walkie-talkies is similar to the effect the villanelle produces in the reader-listener. Just as we listen to echoes, indulging the desire to hear again what we just said that sounds somehow different, when we recite prayers and mantras, we're seeking that blessed moment when the words we speak, chant, or sing come back to us, but more beautiful and wisdom-fragrant.

The love of echoes is a love of mystery and the ever-evolving, transfigured voice. It's a love of the big room or cave you just have to explore. It's the love of the soothing racket you find in a conch shell that you pick up and press to your ear at the beach. It's a love of old barns and the vast, starry night, and it's the sound of liturgy, of mantra. It is an effect on the ear and the human heart. Villanelles are well suited to a meditation on mystery, listening, forgiveness, grace, and goodbye.

The first line of a villanelle is repeated three times. It recurs in the sixth line, the twelfth line, and the eighteenth line. The third line repeats in the ninth and fifteenth lines, and in the nineteenth and final line.

Many poets have said, often ruefully, that a villanelle is an easy poem to write as long as you come up with two great lines, which is easier said than done. Yet it is not impossible. This form, like the couplet, playfully and defiantly celebrates our preoccupation with pairs, and mentors its practitioners in subtlety and musicality.

The villanelle can lend itself rather easily to light verse, but the best examples are more ambitious, opening doors that we have overlooked or never considered before. This famous poem by Dylan Thomas provides a compelling example.

Do Not Go Gentle into That Good Night

Do not go gentle into that good night.
Old age should burn and rave at close of day;
Rage, rage against the dying of the light.

Though wise men at their end know dark is right,
Because their words had forked no lightning they
Do not go gentle into that good night.

Good men, the last wave by, crying how bright
Their frail deeds might have danced in a green bay,
Rage, rage against the dying of the light.

Wild men who caught and sang the sun in flight,
And learn, too late, they grieved it on its way,
Do not go gentle into that good night.

Grave men, near death, who see with blinding sight
Blind eyes could blaze like meteors and be gay,
Rage, rage against the dying of the light.

And you, my father, there on the sad height,
Curse, bless, me now with your fierce tears, I pray.
Do not go gentle into that good night.
Rage, rage against the dying of the light.

Certainly, this is a poem of majestic music and deep feeling. It is a spectacular poem for a spiritual practice on goodbye, death, and letting go. The imminent death of the speaker's father provides the poem's occasion. The poem's speaker exhorts his father to be passionate and defiant to the end, even beyond the end. In Thomas's hands, the demanding rules of the villanelle provide a perfect way to express exquisite grief, a rebuttal to death's finality. It's a moment in which the poet has the last word.

In a real sense, the poetry form itself mentors us in shaping our raw emotions. It helps us aspire to, and sometimes achieve, an eloquent, memorable expression of our most bottled up, powerful emotions.

Exercise: Fun with Mentors

Villanelles as light verse at times can be quite entertaining. Recalling that poetry is also supposed to be fun and a form of play, let's subvert Dylan Thomas's two great lines in this way: *Do not rub gently with that handiwipe./Rage, rage against the rusting of the pipe.* Using these as your first and third lines, try to write a goofy villanelle. Give yourself permission to have fun!

Here is a lighthearted example, apologies to Dylan Thomas, from Carol Aronoff of Hawaii:

Clean Villanelle

Do not rub gently with that handiwipe.
Wash with the fervor of Lady MacBeth.
Rage, rage against the rusting of the pipe.

It's not enough to give a wipe,
to clear your glasses with your breath.
Do not rub gently with that handiwipe.

Though Mr. Clean's a stereotype,
he'll leave your kitchen spotless, fresh.
Rage, rage against the rusting of the pipe.

At times you'll feel like a guttersnipe,
attacking the plumbing until you sweat.
Do not rub gently with that handiwipe.

The virginal maiden, an archetype,
is innocent, rust-free, pure unto death.
Rage, rage against the rusting of the pipe.

This villanelle might seem quite trite,
Though a plumber would say its advice is best.
Do not rub gently with that handiwipe.
Rage, rage against the rusting of the pipe.

Exercise: Nothing Boring in Poetry!
The Texas poet R. S. Gwynn, perhaps our greatest satirist in verse, likes to remind his students that the villanelle works for "boring" subjects—like working at McDonald's. His poem about a woman who wrote a poem a day for syndication is a good example.

Optimist

Villanelle follows sonnet, day by day,
Like multi-colored bon-bons on a plate.
Fridays bring fishcakes and a triolet.

Your scattered rosebuds falling where they may,
Drifting away like every ripped off date,
Villanelle follows sonnet, day by day.

The stacks of yellow foolscap mount. Can they
Confess their fiery mildness of your fate?
Fridays bring fishcakes and a triolet

While aches and years are gathered in the gray
That spreads from roots to ends: your husband's late.
Villanelle follows sonnet, day by day,

And soon enough a world has spun away
Like headlines whirling at a heady rate.
Fridays bring fishcakes and a triolet;

Mondays start the round again: you say,
The camphor gaily blooms beside my gate.
Villanelle follows sonnet, day by day.
Fridays bring fishcakes and a triolet.

Think of something really boring you have done. Worked a booth at a county fair? Collected newspapers all day for a paper drive? Painted a house? Done large loads of laundry? Come up with two rhyming lines that encompass the experience. Allow those lines to be your springboard to creating a villanelle that deals with the experience.

In your journal, write about how the poem you created has helped your spiritual practice as you consider patience, calm abiding, irritation, judgments.

Exercise: Word Golf

"Word golf" is another favorite R. S. Gwynn exercise. For example, *gold, gild,* and *glad* are words that rhyme; so are *glass, class,* and *close.* Use these two sets of rhyming words to create a villanelle. Here is a useful hint. "I always tell writers," Gwynn says, "to go with the easiest rhymes possible in a villanelle. Otherwise, they'll run out."

Gwynn reminds us that writing poetry can be fun. Here is his zany, scrambled villanelle, the inspiration for which the poet Donald Justice describes in a note that seems longer than the poem!

Ellenalliv for Lew: On His Retirement

In graduate school Lew Turco was the champion of two parlor tricks for which alone we would never have forgotten him, even if he had written nothing: one was the trick of being able to recite anything backwards, and to do it instantly; the second and more impressive was the trick of improvising on the spot a Dylan Thomas poem, not every one we could quite remember, though each new Turco-Thomas poem did sound at least faintly familiar and certainly authentic.

Retirement into gentle go not do.
Dies he until stops never poet a.
Do to tasks undone many have still you.

Start they what of half finish ever few.
You with compared they're when away fade they.
Retirement into gentle go not do.

Renown first their on rested have some, true.
Promises early to up live few, hey!
Do to tasks undone many have still you.

Writes who man the to given be must due.
Does he what for reward small too is pay.
Retirement into gentle go not do.

Yield to not and, find to, seek to, strive to.
Truth its holds still saw ancient this that pray.
Do to tasks undone many have still you.

Sleep you before go to miles have you, Lew.
Forth travel you may so, anew breaks day.
Retirement into gentle go not do.
Do to tasks undone many have still you.

Exercise: Line Prompts

On a more serious note, use the following as your first and third lines in a villanelle: *At last I see myself the sum of twos. I split myself by listening to the blues.* Let the lines themselves suggest where you should go in your poem.

The Welsh poet-professor Tony Curtis, who writes villanelles and teaches them, has said of the form, "the only justification for seriously attempting a villanelle is that the subject matter and one's emotional and spiritual response to an experience may be best served by the form. Our thought and feelings are drawn to its unique weaving of words, its mantra-like key couplet. That couplet, formed by the first and third lines, is thereafter kept apart by the second line's rhyme for another five trios, until, with a flourish, the poem concludes with those two lines brought together as the couplet we'd always known them to be. It's a dance of words, two lovers parted and meeting again at the end of the film. It is very, very satisfying."

Curtis effectively expresses the villanelle's link to intimacy and devotion. Here is the late Canadian poet and jurist F. R. Scott's *Villanelle for Our Time*, which singer-songwriter Leonard Cohen set to music on his 2004 album *Dear Heather*.

> From bitter searching of the heart,
> Quickened with passion and with pain
> We rise to play a greater part.
> This is the faith from which we start:
> Men shall know commonwealth again
> From bitter searching of the heart.
> We loved the easy and the smart,
> But now, with keener hand and brain,
> We rise to play a greater part.

The lesser loyalties depart,
And neither race nor creed remain
From bitter searching of the heart.
Not steering by the venal chart
That tricked the mass for private gain,
We rise to play a greater part.
Reshaping narrow law and art
Whose symbols are the millions slain,
From bitter searching of the heart
We rise to play a greater part.

I did not know this poem until I listened to it on Cohen's album. I thought it was the most exquisite, memorable 9/11 poem I'd heard, and when I discovered that it had been written long before the event, I marveled once again at the timelessness of art. It powerfully expresses two truths that many of us think of as lessons of 9/11: our world for a time will seem more frightening and uncertain, yet humanity will recover, survive, and evolve. For me, the poem evokes the knee-buckling sadness of that day, and also the stillness immediately after—the hours when there were no planes in the sky, when people worldwide reached out with compassion to our country, when a million Iraqis held candles and sadly marched through the streets of Baghdad. The poem articulates the opportunity that a terrible event created for worldwide spiritual growth. And even if our leaders miserably failed to comprehend or act on that opportunity, countless individuals everywhere have done so. All of that is said so poignantly in nineteen deceptively simple lines. That's the beauty of spiritual poetry practice.

Here is another example of a resonant villanelle. The author of *The House on the Hill*, Edwin Arlington Robinson, is one of the great American masters of poetry and storytelling. In his lifetime, he was also immensely popular and accessible. More than once, his books of poetry were bestsellers.

They are all gone away,
The House is shut and still,
There is nothing more to say.

Through broken walls and gray
The winds blow bleak and shrill:
They are all gone away.

Nor is there one to-day
To speak them good or ill:
There is nothing more to say.

Why is it then we stray
Around the sunken sill?
They are all gone away,

And our poor fancy-play
For them is wasted skill:
There is nothing more to say.

There is ruin and decay
In the House on the Hill:
They are all gone away,
There is nothing more to say.

Collaborative Exercise: Tune In to Others

Compose the first line of a villanelle while a friend composes the third line. Alternate writing the rest of the lines of the poem. Repeat this exercise at least three times.

The rondeau and the rondel are two French forms that are similar to the villanelle. Let's have a look at them.

Rondeau

Like the villanelle, the rondeau makes use of two rhymes throughout. Fifteen lines in length, the poem is divided into three stanzas. The first stanza consists of five lines (a quintet), the middle stanza consists of four lines (a quatrain), and the third stanza consists of six lines (a sestet). The ninth and fifteenth lines are shorter and contain the first phrase of line one. Throughout the form's long history, these rules of circling back, of line repetition, have remained remarkably constant. Traditional stanza alignment and rhyme follow this pattern: AABBA AABR AABBAR. Here is an example by Austin Dobson.

With Pipe and Flute

With pipe and flute the rustic Pan
Of old made music sweet for man;
    And wonder hushed the warbling bird,
    And closer drew the calm-eyed herd,—
The rolling river slowlier ran.

Ah! would,—ah! would, a little span
Some air of Arcady could fan
    This age of ours, too seldom stirred
      With pipe and flute!

But now for gold we plot and plan;
And from Beersheba unto Dan
    Apollo's self might pass unheard.
    Or find the night-jar's note preferred,—
Not so it fared when time began
        With pipe and flute!

For many of us in our time, the sense of this poem is not very seductive. But the music created by the form itself is oddly compelling. There is sense, *and* there is no sense, and both are simultaneously true, a Taoist might remind us. In hearing certain tones and melodies, perhaps we take in, or dredge up in ourselves, meanings and feelings that literal words alone do not reveal to us. Perhaps that is why we listen to a favorite song over and over again, even singing along once we get the words. Perhaps that is the beauty of form, a sickle against the Gordian Knot that binds our deepest feelings, questions, and desires.

Exercise: Refrain Prompts
Begin a poem with the words *I rise up and my head. I rise up* is your refrain. Base your other rhyme on *bored.* For example:

I rise up and my head
        red
        bored
        word
        instead

        fled
        dread
        admired

I rise up

> coasted
> bread
> roasted
> cord
> dead

I rise up

Fill in the incomplete lines. There! We have collaborated on a rondeau. Now try one from scratch, on your own. All you need to begin is a first line, and a second rhyme.

Rondel

The rondel contains thirteen lines and employs only two rhymes. Your first two lines are very important, because they must be repeated, sometimes with slight variations, as lines seven and eight, and once more as lines twelve and thirteen. Here is an anonymous example.

I wish I had more money
Than tea and honey.
I wish I had a ring,
A friend to sing

To in this cold valley
Where frost is king.
I wish that I could sing
Of tea and honey.

It isn't funny,
Like no dressing

On a sore. I'm lonely.
I wish I had more money
Than tea and honey.

The rhymes can fall into any pattern you choose.

Another variation of this form, called the rondel supreme, resembles even more closely the sonnet. It consists of fourteen lines (two quatrains and a sestet) and the rhyme scheme ABBA ABAB ABBAAB. The first two lines of stanza one are repeated (a refrain) at the end of stanzas two and three. Here is an example by the fifteenth-century Anglo-Norman poet Charles d'Orléans:

Confessional

My ghostly father, let me confess,
First to God and then to you,
That at a window—do you know how?—
I stole a kiss of great sweetness.

It was done without advisedness,
But it is done, not undone now.
My ghostly father, let me confess,
First to God and then to you.

But it shall be restored, doubtless,
For kisses one should rebestow,
And that to God I make this vow,
Otherwise, I ask forgiveness.
My ghostly father, let me confess,
First to God and then to you.

Exercise: Two Lines, Then on Your Own

Try writing your own rondel by building on these first and second lines: *I cannot make the grade/Unless I learn from you.* Remember that you can incorporate slight variations in the refrain lines. In other words, the lines need not be repeated verbatim. Always try to be receptive to the intimacy of your inquiry, and to the breakthroughs you may at any moment experience.

11

Sestina:
Repetition in Practice

In twelfth-century Europe, wandering singers and storytellers called troubadours lived a romantic existence, making their living in villages and towns by singing songs and telling stories that preserved history and entertained listeners. They are responsible for the forms with which we have been working—villanelle, rondeau, rondel—as well as the longer, and perhaps most challenging, intricate form, the sestina.

The word *sestina* comes from the Italian *sesto*, meaning "sixth" (from the Latin root *sextus*). The poem consists of six stanzas of six lines each, followed by an envoy of three lines (in other words, a stanza of three lines). Once again we meet the mathematic beauty of a compelling poetry form based on an arrangement of threes. The success of the sestina depends largely on the poet's skill in repeating the end words of the first stanza in every stanza that follows, including the envoy. As with the other forms we've met, the repetition, though tricky, aids memorization and performance when well executed. Like a benevolent language tic, it triggers the brain and lodges pleasurably in the ear.

So that we may get a bead on how the sestina's end-word repetitions work, let's take a look at a poem I wrote in tribute to grandparents and an aunt I never knew.

In 1916, my infant mother, her parents, and older sister fled Austria and the First World War and settled in Cleveland, Ohio. Both parents died as a result of the influenza epidemic of the time. A few years later, my mother's sister also died of the flu. Thus, by the age of five, my mother was an orphan, raised by nuns in a convent when she wasn't cycling through abusive foster families.

It was forty-nine years, and almost twenty-five years after my mother's death, before I could write a poem about a drama that so thoroughly altered my family history. To my surprise, when I found that I was writing such a poem, I realized it was in the form of a sestina. Perhaps the weight and dignity of the form seemed appropriate to the occasion. Spiritually, perhaps, I needed the form to balance and contain emotions I experienced as I relived my family's trials. When I contemplate grief, loss, and endurance, my practice of prayers and prostrations includes this poem.

Epidemic: 1918

I'd give my soul, and all I own, for food.
My sister shivers in bed, her bear the flu
That sleeps with so many this year. Our name is Winter.
Our parents go. Like figures on a cake,
They are so stiff they cannot bend to offer
Comfort or a cure for sister's sake.

I sit alone, hugging my knees that shake
While sister moans. She turns away from food
Our starving neighbor in her kindness offers,

Who lost two children of her own to flu.
I wish I could console her, give her cake
To blunt her hunger and erase a winter

She will not forget. It's always winter
Where we cower, praying to forsake
The awful hand that holds the arsenic cake.
I'm dying for a snack, a bit of food.
Our neighbor pokes the embers, closes the flue
As if to say *I've only ashes to offer*

Gods who laugh at us and never proffer
Anything we need. But endless winter
Is abundant, spreading its icy flow
Until our patience breaks. *For goodness sake*,
We cry, then double over from lack of food.
It's rich, but what we wouldn't give for cake.

I'm sick of feeling death, this bellyache.
Somebody has to show with a better offer,
Maybe Red Cross units with healthy food.
But who am I kidding? It's bleak. It's gruesome winter.
No one's coming, nothing to sponge this ache
Out of our hearts. Instead, my sister flew

Away. There's nothing but the end, the flu
That banishes all hope, all dreams of cake,
And bears us far away for its master's sake.
Nothing we say, no ransom we might offer
Changes into spring eternal winter,
Or piles our barren board with exotic foods.

Sister, may the afterlife be food,
A piece of cake. May godforsaken flu
Be obsolete, and winter a lover's offer.

Our third guest author, the poet Diane Thiel, teaches at the
University of New Mexico. She shares her thoughts on the ses-
tina, suggests some useful exercises she has employed in work-
shops, and graciously offers a sestina of her own. Here is Diane
in her own words:

"The repeated words create a rhyme-like effect that occurs at
seemingly unpredictable intervals as the pattern changes from
stanza to stanza. The poem then ends with a three-line stanza,
with each line containing two of the words (ABCDEF/FAEBDC/
CFDABE/ECBFAD/DEACFB/BDFECA/AB,CD,EF).

"When used to the poem's advantage, the repetitions cre-
ate a forward movement, and the words serve different func-
tions in the progression of the poem. They might also create a
cyclical effect. The repetitions might also serve an important
thematic purpose. In *Love Letters*, the closed-in nature of the
family home and the relationship being described find a match
with the closed-in repetitive form of the sestina."

Love Letters

My mother wanted to learn some German
for my father and because her children
could already speak it a little.
She was tired of dusting the stacks of books
she couldn't read, tired of the letters
she always had to ask me to translate.

He was usually willing to translate
the cards his mother had written in German.
But sometimes there were other letters,
and when he read them to her and the children,
she had the same feeling she'd had with books
before she learned to read, when she was little.

She said it bothered her a little
that her own children would have to translate
for her, that they could pick up the same books
that were as Greek to her as they were German.
She started learning it from her children
and decided to leave my father letters.

She wrote my father daily love letters
and carefully placed them on the little
table where they put things for the children,
next to our favorite set of translations
of fairy tales we first heard in German.
She leaned one every day against his books,

the white paper stark beside the dark books.
But my father never answered her letters.
Instead, he returned them with his German
corrections in the margin, his little
red marks—hieroglyphs for her to translate,
as if she were one of the children.

Maybe she was just one of the children
in that house surrounded by rows of books.

Maybe her whole life was a translation
of what she imagined in the letters.
The space between them made her that little
girl, wandering lost inside the German.

Because her own children were half-German,
she built her life around those little books
translating the lines of her own letters.

(Diane Thiel)

Thiel's sestina is a wonderful poem to reflect on during the contemplation of any problems you have in communicating with loved ones—or with the messages of a higher power.

Diane Thiel's Recommended Exercises

Exercise: Use a Writer-Mentor
"Adopt (and adapt) six words from a writer who has influenced you. Give credit to your source. Use them to write an homage, perhaps. Donald Justice did this in his *Sestina on Six Words by Weldon Kees*."

Exercise: Shift at the Center
"Though it may be easy to follow the rules and "fill in the blanks" to create a passable sestina, writing a good one isn't easy! Sestinas tend to lag midway, and a good one needs a serious charge or turn of events, perhaps a twist that only a good story provides. Try to choose a subject that will have some shift at its center."

Exercise: A Sestria, Perhaps?

"Since many sestinas lag, the form might provide a good opportunity to "invent" a new form. Use the concept and pattern of repetition, but try a half sestina; invent a *sestria*, perhaps.

"A variation on the sestina can be found in the rondeau redoubled, which consists of five stanzas of four lines each and a closing five-line stanza. Here is an example by the marvelous poet and educator Lewis Turco cited in his *Book of Forms: A Handbook of Poetics.*

from *Bordello*

Suddenly, nothing was left of all those
years we'd spent together in the same house,
under that old mansard that bent and rose
above us, gracefully guarding. The spruce

in the dooryard spired out of the grass
like a steeple, pulling us taut as bows—
both generations. But age is a noose:
suddenly, nothing was left of all those

mornings and nights. I, Jason Potter, chose
to lay away my helpmeet and my spouse
in a lone bed. So ended my repose.
Years we'd spent together in the same house

became beads to tell, the string broken—loose
time come unstrung. Still, outside, the spruce grows,
and it is nature to try to mend loss.
Under that old mansard that bent and rose

over the life we'd built, my blood still flows
in fever now and then. I make my truce
with flesh through these paid women whom I use.
Above us, guarding and graceful, the spruce

used to seem a symbol of common use
and fulfillment of self and heart—those blues
tipping sheer limbs sharply; strong and close
and clean, the bole and needles of pure hues . . .
Suddenly, nothing was left.

"Notice how the lines of stanza one progressively end succeeding stanzas (line one ends stanza two, line two ends stanza three, and so on.)"

Collaborative Exercise: Writing the Group Sestina
Choose six words and write them out for each member of your group. Or use a board and set up a *grid* for the poem. Participants may call out lines that end with the appropriate words. Have fun with this exercise and don't be hard on yourself. Your group may not produce a great sestina, but you may well write several interesting lines. You will certainly enhance your understanding of the form.

The possibilities of the sestina, like any form in poetry, are limited only by your imagination. The poet James Cummins has even written a book of connected sestinas based on the Perry Mason characters. Here is the fourth sestina from *The Whole Truth*.

"Perry—" Furious, Mason looked up from the chess
Game he played with himself every night. His mother

Loomed in the doorway, leaning grimly on her walker.
"Perry, turn up the heat? Please? Your father—"
"—Is dead!" Perry raged, his bitter voice rammed
Into the old crone's face. "If you were ambulatory—"

Mason bit it off. He was lucky she was ambulatory
At all, considering the wheezes and grunts her chest
Made, fixing her milk, or peeing: sounds that rammed
Into his skull with all the force of a mother's—!
Forget it! But did she have to bring up his father,
How he'd go prowling at night for a streetwalker—

Somebody who can work her legs without a walker!—
How little Perry would watch another barely ambulatory
Schizophrenic barely climb the stairway, while his father
Made growling noises at her shoes, or rubbed her chest.
He couldn't distinguish: father, stairs, whore, mother . . .
Next day at the shopping mall, pushing her up a ramp,

Then alongside the windows, and down another ramp,
Mason thought of the Hitchcock film with Robert Walker:
The pact made to exchange murders . . . Until his mother
Interrupted his thoughts. "I remember being ambulatory.
Before your father—" But her throat caught, her chest
Heaving around that old heart, broken by his father . . .

Like a stake, she drove home her hatred of his father.
"He'd bruise me where it didn't show—watch that ramp!—
And ran around with a stripper named 'Community Chest'—
They'd get so tanked up on that damned Johnny Walker—
Until they were both slobbering, just barely ambulatory—!"
She broke down, sobbing. "Perry, I'm not your mother . . .

Hasn't it dawned on you I'm too old to be your mother?
Think back, my baby, try: don't you remember your father
Looming over a woman, her neck broken? The ambulance
   story,
That she fell—" The wheelchair slipped away down a ramp.
Dazed, Mason watched his grandmother shriek, other
   walkers
Scatter, as that cage hit a truck. He grabbed his chest . . .

Ampules, laboratory, tubes forming a ramp from his chest
To some dials. Mason saw himself hunched over a walker
In a courtroom, pleading his case to his mother and father.

Notice with what brilliant cleverness Cummins distorts the
repetition of *ambulatory* in stanza five, changing it to *ambu-*
lance story. This is just one of many examples of inventiveness
that surprises us and enriches our experience of the poem.

This is what we hope for in every poem we read, write, and
draw on in our practice. The sestina, more expansive than the
villanelle, allows us more space in practice within the inevi-
table repetitions. In this way it more closely resembles the call-
and-response exchange we experience with a spiritual lama,
rabbi, priest, or pastor. This poem by Algernon Charles Swin-
burne illustrates the sestina's appeal in spiritual practice.

I saw my soul at rest upon a day
     As a bird sleeping in the nest of night,
Among soft leaves that give the starlight way
     To touch its wings but not its eyes with light;
So that it knew as one in visions may,
     And knew not as men waking, of delight.

This was the measure of my soul's delight;
    It had no power of joy to fly by day,
Nor part in the large lordship of the light;
    But in a secret moon-beholden way
Had all its will of dreams and pleasant night,
    And all the love and life that sleepers may.

But such life's triumph as men waking may
    It might not have to feed its faint delight
Between the stars by night and sun by day,
    Shut up with green leaves and a little light;
Because its way was as a lost star's way,
    A world's not wholly known of day or night.

All loves and dreams and sounds and gleams of night
    Made it all music that such minstrels may,
And all they had they gave it of delight;
    But in the full face of the fire of day
What place shall be for any starry light,
    What part of heaven in all the wide sun's way?

Yet the soul woke not, sleeping by the way,
    Watched as a nursling of the large-eyed night,
And sought no strength nor knowledge of the day,
    Nor closer touch conclusive of delight,
Nor mightier joy nor truer than dreamers may,
    Nor more of song than they, nor more of light.

For who sleeps once and sees the secret light
    Whereby sleep shows the soul a fairer way
Between the rise and rest of day and night,

Shall care no more to fare as all men may,
But be his place of pain or of delight,
     There shall he dwell, beholding night as day.

Song, have thy day and take thy fill of light
     Before the night be fallen across thy way;
          Sing while he may, man hath no long delight.

12

Limerick and Epigram:
Playful and Laughing

Poetry is many things, and one of them is fun. Our spiritual practice should also be joyous, containing vibrant elements of fun. So, perhaps we should call limericks and epigrams the fun forms. Poetry can be the catalyst for laughter's sweet release, and poems in these forms fit perfectly in practice on joy and play. These forms certainly possess an innate ability to tickle us.

Limerick

The origin of the limerick is disputed to this day. We know that it came into being some time after Chaucer's fourteenth century, though it would be no great surprise, if we took a time machine back through history, to discover that Chaucer's ribald humor was in fact the model for early practitioners of the form. Some believe it is a French form, while others claim its ancestry is English or Irish. What we do agree on is that the limerick's vast popularity today can be traced to one book, Edward Lear's *Book of Nonsense*, published in 1846.

The limerick is a popular form of light verse (verse that is not outwardly serious; verse that primarily intends to entertain), and is the close cousin of the pun. Limericks even appear in operettas, as in this bit from Gilbert and Sullivan:

My name is John Wellington Wells.
I'm a dealer in magic and spells,
In blessings and curses
And ever-filled purses
In prophecies, witches and knells.

Even Web sites have been devoted exclusively to the form. The home page of one recently expired site offered the following encouragement.

If you would like to make life lighter,
Or someone's day a little brighter
You're in the right place,
Smile a happy face
And check out the limerickwriter.

Entertain with a poetic toast,
Or be heard as a creative host
Get a limerick here
For your listener's ear—
You can even use one for a roast!

Want to spice up a business lunch?
Regale friends at a Sunday brunch?
We provide you rhymes
For fun and good times,
And for poems that pack a big punch.

The limerick is a five-line stanza (a quintet) with a rhyme scheme of AABBA. The first, second, and fifth lines consist of an iambic foot (an unstressed syllable followed by a stressed syllable), then two anapestic feet (two unstressed syllables followed by a stressed syllable). Lines three and four can consist of either two anapests, or an iamb followed by an anapest. Here is an anonymous example:

There once was a man from Nantucket
Who kept all his cash in a bucket;
    But his daughter named Nan
    Ran away with a man,
And as for the bucket, Nantucket.

This poem is unlikely to solve the world's great mysteries or increase our chances for prosperity, but I have experimented with limericks as part of my daily spiritual practice, especially when I find I am feeling *too* serious or dour. Here are two of my trusted allies in practice:

Each morning I ask to be open
Sometimes I pray that it's fun
Whether it is or it's not,
I've got what I've got—
Desire to wake up and open.

*

Where is it, Robert—compassion?
Are you distracted today by fashion,
What's pretty, what's rad,
What's chic or what's bad?
Where is it, Robert—compassion?

In this way, I lighten my practice and introduce the element of healing through laughter. Again, intention is everything. With the proper intention, limericks will not be distracting. Their sheer cleverness and nonsense make us smile. Many poems suffer worse fates!

Exercise: Beginnings and Endings
Take the first and fifth lines that follow and complete the limerick:

> The hairdresser's effort looks awful ...
> She's sorry her hair is such trouble.

Exercise: Prime Cuts
Many limericks are quite bawdy. Try your hand at a limerick that critiques a love relationship you are familiar with. For example, consider this anonymous effort:

A Butcher

There once was a butcher named Simms
Who married a woman of whims.
   She said "No!" once too often,
   So he purchased a coffin
And made farewell love to her limbs.

Make an attempt at composing limericks for half a dozen relationships you are familiar with (yes, you can write about one or more of your own!). Poking fun at yourself can be quite therapeutic.

Collaborative Exercise: Round and Round You Go
Work with one friend, or with four. If you choose to work with one, write alternating lines for six limericks. If you work

with four partners, then each poet shall compose one line. Create six limericks in this fashion.

Epigram

What is an Epigram? A dwarfish whole;
It's body brevity, and wit its soul.
   (Samuel Taylor Coleridge)

Have you ever been at a party and felt dull-witted and tongue-tied? Hours later, did you think of the effervescent retort to something someone said? So many perfect comebacks are a day late.

Well, all is not lost. The epigram is a form in poetry that allows us to get it right. Originating with the ancient Greeks, it often rhymes, is very short, and can be witty, devotional, vicious, satiric, sarcastic. Its brevity is its armor and its razor's edge. As in the delicious response, the epigram always has a sharp point. The following Alexander Pope epigram could be part of a revealing exchange between two contemporary, favor-trading professionals at a convention:

I am His Highness' dog at Kew;
Pray tell me, sir, whose dog are you?

Noted practitioners of the form include John Donne, Robert Herrick, Matthew Prior, Ezra Pound, and Robert Frost. There is even a Web site, www.logopoeia.com/ed, that enlists a computer program to glean thousands of epigrams from the poems of Emily Dickinson.

Here are some poems by the Roman poet Martial, translated by J. V. Cunningham, himself a master of the form.

Sabinus, I don't like you. You know why?
Sabinus, I don't like you. That is why.

*

You write, you tell me, for posterity.
May you be read, my friend, immediately.

*

Believe me, sir, I'd like to spend whole days,
Yes, and whole evenings in your company,
But the two miles between your house and mine
Are four miles when I go there to come back.
You're seldom home, and when you are deny it,
Engrossed with business or with yourself.
Now, I don't mind the two-mile trip to see you;
What I do mind is going four to not to.

Exercise: The Withering Word
Think of five people in your life who have embarrassed you.
Compose an epigrammatic couplet for each of them. Next,
compose five epigrams for the same five people, but insist that
compassion be your guide. The first five epigrams you write
for this exercise clean out your system, removing self-erected
obstacles; the second five are epigrams you may add to your
spiritual practice.

Exercise: One-Line Prompts
Complete the epigrams using the following lines as starting
points. Yes, you may exceed two lines.

I'm weary of your critical chatter ...

When you are old but not quite dead ...

I saw you in the supermarket yesterday ...

The phone rang. Its ringing drove me batty ...

When you drove off, leaving me at 7-Eleven ...

Grant me the patience to stand in the subway ...

Have I ever told you that I find you ...

Your mother called to tell you off ...

If God will visit me tonight ...

If only I could be someone I'm not ...

Collaborative Exercise: Babbling Cross-Talk

Pair up with someone. Trade off in composing epigrammatic couplets. For example, you write the first line, your partner writes the second; then your partner writes the first line, you the second, and so on, until you've created a wonderful, biting, witty epigrammatic chain.

As with haiku and other minimalist forms, the limerick and the epigram place a high premium on brevity and keen observation. There is no place for the fuzzy thinker to hide. These attributes alone make both forms friendly to spiritual practice. Try them and see.

13

Ghazal:
Attention and Wonder

Separation

None but me may be broken by the woes of separation;
My life ends desolated by the throes of separation.

Exhausted stranger, lover, spent beggar, mind-addled one;
I've endured the burden of fortune, the blows of separation.

If separation turns up in my hand I will kill it;
Tearful and bloody I'll pay my dues of separation.

Where do I go, what should I do? Who will I confess to?
Who grants justice, who pays the bill of separation?

In the pain of separation not a moment's peace is mine;
For God's sake, be just, pay the dues of separation.

Separated from Your Presence I'll make separation sick,
Until my heart's blood spurts from my eyes of separation.

Where am I? What makes this separation and grief?
Was I born for grief that grows of separation?

So it goes. Day and night, branded by love, like Hafiz,
With dawn's nightingales, I weep songs of woe, of separation.

   (Hafiz, trans. Robert McDowell)

Iran is the birthplace of a verse form known as the ghazal
(pronounced *guzzle*, rhymes with *puzzle*). It means "conversing with women" and evolved in the tenth century A.D. from a Persian form known as qasida. Hafiz, who lived in the fourteenth century, was Persia's most famous poet and practitioner of the ghazal.

The mobile ghazal migrated to India in the twelfth century, then into Pakistan and points west. Goethe loved the form, and through his efforts the ghazal became popular in nineteenth-century Germany. Today, Pakistani and Indian ghazal singers rival in popularity our *American Idol* finalists. Here is a ghazal by Goethe that loosely follows the original form. Many early western poets and translators did not attempt faithful renditions of the form's rhyming patterns.

The Unlimited

That thou can't never end, doth make thee great,
And that thou ne'er beginnest, is thy fate.
Thy song is changeful as yon starry frame,
End and beginning evermore the same;
And what the middle bringeth, but contains
What was at first, and what at last remains.
Thou art of joy the true and minstrel-source,
From thee pours wave on wave with ceaseless force.

A mouth that's aye prepared to kiss,

A breast whence flows a loving song,
A throat that finds no draught amiss,

An open heart that knows no wrong.

And what though all the world should sink!

Hafis, with thee, alone with thee

Will I contend! joy, misery,

The portion of us twain shall be;
Like thee to love, like thee to drink,—

This be my pride,—this, life to me!

Now, Song, with thine own fire be sung,—
For thou art older, thou more young!

The ghazal in its concentration is like a fragrant, exotic scent. In its independence and single-mindedness, it suggests the haiku and the epigraph. The poet Agha Shahid Ali spoke of the "wonderful pleasure of immediate recognition which is central to the ghazal," as in "Beloved, You open the sky to me / and straighten out the road that I may come to you." The beloved is always a metaphor for God or a higher power, so we immediately respond to lines like these on both a worldly and spiritual level. Like feminine energy, the ghazal is a true force of nature. It is effective in a practice in which you are meditating or praying about peace, authenticity, and wonder.

The ghazal traditionally consists of five to fifteen couplets (called *sher*)—no less and no more. There must be no enjambment between couplets. Each one must be able to stand alone. Like the fabled Women in Black who silently stand together in public places to protest war, each couplet is significant and memorable in its autonomy; together, they may combine in an electric experience that rewards extended contemplation, but as K. C. Kanda points out in *Masterpieces of Urdu Ghazal: From the 17th to the 20th Century*, "The different couplets of the ghazal are not bound by the unity and consistency of thought. Each couplet is a self-sufficient unit, detachable and quotable, generally containing the complete expression of an idea."

In its native Persian and Urdu, each line of every couplet is written in the same meter. It's possible to do this in English, too, though most ghazals by American poets do not attempt it. Instead, our practitioners often compose lines of roughly the same length. Given that so many American poems are written in free verse, this decision makes good horse sense.

Whether you are writing your ghazal in strict meter or in lines of approximate equal length, the poem always begins with a rhyming couplet (*matla*) and refrain (*radif*). This rhyme must be repeated at the end of the second line of each couplet that follows. Thus the rhyming pattern looks like this: AA BA CA DA EA FA GA and on to the end. The pattern of each ghazal is identified in its first couplet, as both the recurrent rhyme and refrain are determined there like the refrain in the sestina and villanelle.

Finally, the poet "signs" the poem in the last couplet (*makhta*), using her or his real name or pen name.

Here is an example by Agha Shahid Ali (spun off from one line of a poem by Laurence Hope). Following the second line of each stanza, I've taken the liberty of including in parentheses the rhyme scheme. I have also underlined the interior rhymes preceding the refrain.

Pale hands I loved beside the Shalimar

Where are you now? Who lies beneath your <u>spell</u> tonight
before you agonize him in <u>farewell</u> tonight? (AA)

Pale hands that once loved me beside the Shalimar:
Whom else from rapture's road will you <u>expel</u> tonight? (BA)

Those "Fabrics of Cashmere—""to make Me beautiful—"
"Trinket"—to gem—"Me to adorn—How—<u>tell</u>"—tonight? (CA)

I beg for haven: Prisons, let open your gates—
A refugee from pity seeks a <u>cell</u> tonight. (DA)

Lord, cried out the idols, *Don't let us be broken:
Only we can convert the* <u>infidel</u> tonight. (EA)

In the heart's veined temple all statues have been smashed.
No priest in saffron's left to toll its <u>knell</u> tonight. (FA)

And I, Shahid, only am escaped to <u>tell</u> thee—
God sobs in my arms. Call me <u>Ishmael</u> tonight. (GA)

The wordplay (*infidel/cell*, and my favorite, *Ishmael*) and mentor play (quotes from Emily Dickinson and Herman Melville) are abundant in this poem. In fact, one can scarcely imagine it without these qualities. The poem even makes an effort to satisfy the form's ancient thematic requirement—unrequited love. More to the point, the subject of the earliest ghazals was love of a higher being, God. Thus the form becomes an expression of highly developed devotion, and one can readily imagine the poet as pilgrim offering his gift, his alms.

Some believe that it is impossible to understand and appreciate ghazals without having awareness of at least some of Sufism's concepts. A mystical branch of Islam, Sufism is somewhat familiar to many westerners through the poems of Rumi and Hafiz. Most often described as a philosophy or science, the Sufi Way is a path by which the individual may travel to the Divine, purifying inwardly along the way and developing admirable traits (humility, generosity, compassion, and so on).

Exercise: Opening and Closing Couplets

After reading the ghazals included here, take twenty minutes to write at least three opening couplets and three closing couplets. Share your creations with your group or friends. Trade couplets with your peers. Next, create at least three additional couplets (you may write more than three) to complete your ghazal. Share these and discuss them with your peers.

Exercise: Ghazals on the House!

This game requires a good group of friends. Put numbers corresponding to the number of friends in a hat and draw them. The friend who draws number one must compose an opening couplet. Friend number two follows, and so on until everyone has contributed a couplet. The last friend must, of course, compose the last couplet, thereby gaining the privilege and responsibility of including his name or pen name. Read the ghazal to the group, and then discuss its merits and demerits, if any.

Later, make use of the group ghazal in spiritual practice, and all come back together at some point to discuss the experience.

Exercise: All the Ghazals Fit to Print

Newspapers can be excellent sources and inspirations for poetry. Peruse sections of the daily papers and write your own couplets derived from the stories you read. (Headlines can be marvelous starter kits.)

In closing this chapter, here is *Sam's Ghazal*, a contemporary poem by Elise Paschen. Can you guess who Sam is? Do you have a "Sam" in your life? Perhaps he's deserving of a ghazal of your own.

You're out. The house is dead. With me:
you're safe. Why not stay home, instead, with me?

That Ur prince whisked you off past four.
At my leash-end, you're not misled by me.

He's like a tide. He comes. He goes.
I'm always here. Life's anchored with me.

My needs are few: a bowl, a lead, some love.
You won't get in the red with me.

You never have to cook, just pop a Mighty Dog:
a snap to have breakfasted with me.

He paws, he yaps, he barely listens.
I'm all ears. Much is left unsaid with me.

Perhaps I have some quirks (stairs scare, streets clank),
but you have always kept your head with me.

He is six foot one. I am one foot high.
Don't ever let him tread on me.

Though small, I claim my space and like you snug.
(It's tough sharing a bed with me.)

My name is Samson. Yours is Paschen.
So keep your name and stay unwed with me.

14

Pantoum:
Questing, Devotion, Gratitude

Parent's Pantoum

for Maxine Kumin

Where did these enormous children come from,
More ladylike than we have ever been?
Some of ours look older than we feel.
How did they appear in their long dresses

More ladylike than we have ever been?
But they moan about their aging more than we do,
In their fragile heels and long black dresses.
They say they admire our youthful spontaneity.

They moan about their aging more than we do,
A somber group—why don't they brighten up?
Though they say they admire our youthful spontaneity
They beg us to be dignified like them

As they ignore our pleas to brighten up.
Someday perhaps we'll capture their attention
Then we won't try to be dignified like them
Nor they to be so gently patronizing.

Someday perhaps we'll capture their attention.
Don't they know that we're supposed to be the stars?
Instead they are so gently patronizing.
It makes us feel like children—second-childish?

Perhaps we're too accustomed to be stars.
The famous flowers glowing in the garden,
So now we pout like children. Second-childish?
Quaint fragments of forgotten history?

Our daughters stroll together in the garden,
Chatting of news we've chosen to ignore,
Pausing to toss us morsels of their history,
Not questions to which only we know answers.

Eyes closed to news we've chosen to ignore,
We'd rather excavate old memories,
Disdaining age, ignoring pain, avoiding mirrors.
Why do they never listen to our stories?

Because they hate to excavate old memories
They don't believe our stories have an end.
They don't ask questions because they dread the
    answers.
They don't see that we've become their mirrors,

We offspring of our enormous children.
    (Carolyn Kizer)

Solid, elegant yet frugal, the pantoum is a versatile style.

Poetry finds comparisons in dissimilar things. For instance, the poet and insurance executive Wallace Stevens was fond of wearing colorful print ties to his office; he referred to them as "a bit of Florida." By this, he meant that his ties injected a splash of color into the otherwise drab gray-and-white environment of the offices of the Hartford Company. The pantoum provides the same benefit in the world of poetry and spiritual practice.

Poetry's connections to our world are as diverse as the regions of the human brain. I remember fondly the nooks and crannies of the four-square houses I've lived in, the dark wood of the built-in bookcases off the entry, the crafted doodads contributed by each successive owner. Identical are the pleasures of a pantoum with its cyclical quatrains and often dreamy cadences. Its repetitions suggest an intriguing crosstalk with music. In fact, the second movement of Maurice Ravel's Piano Trio in A Minor is named "Pantoum" (*assez vif*).

The pantoum in Malaysia is known as a pantun. The French writer Ernest Fouinet introduced the form in his poems in the nineteenth century, and Victor Hugo (in translations) and Charles Baudelaire made it popular, and eventually accessible to writers in English. Though until recently the pantoum had rarely been adapted to our language, it has been modified by poets of other languages for centuries. Here is one example from Dante's *Divine Comedy*.

> I have seen her walk all dressed in green,
> so formed she would have sparked love in a stone,
> that love I bear for her very shadow,

so that I wished her, in those fields of grass,
as much in love as ever yet was woman,
closed around by all the highest hills.

The rivers will flow upwards to the hills
before this wood, that is so soft and green,
takes fire, as might ever lovely woman,
for me, who would choose to sleep on stone,
all my life, and go eating grass,
only to gaze at where her clothes cast shadow.

Whenever the hills cast blackest shadow,
with her sweet green, the lovely woman
hides it, as a man hides stone in grass.

In its original shape, the form is made up of a series of quatrains that are intertwined by repetition. The second and fourth lines of the first stanza are repeated as the first and third lines of the next stanza. This pattern continues until, in the last stanza, the second and fourth lines repeat the first and third lines of the original stanza. On occasion, this third line may not appear in the closing stanza. If both lines appear there, however, the pleasure of closure, like the click of the lid of W. B. Yeat's exquisitely crafted box, is undeniable. Lines can be of any length, and the form cannot help but encourage word-play and the sporting art of punning.

The pattern looks like this. Each letter of the alphabet that follows calls attention to repetition of a line (not a rhyme, as in other scansions we have done). Keep in mind that the pan-toum is composed in quatrains.

Line 1	A
Line 2	B
Line 3	C
Line 4	D

Line 5	B
Line 6	E
Line 7	D
Line 8	F

Line 9	E
Line 10	G
Line 11	F
Line 12	H

Line 13	G
Line 14	I
Line 15	H
Line 16	J

In the form's classic rendition, the poem's first line appears as the final quatrain's last line; the poem's third line may often appear as the final stanza's second line.

This elemental form mirrors nature itself, creating its own space. That is why pantoums work well in meditations or prayers that concentrate on devotion, gratitude, and kindness, or questing and zeal. Here is an example by Anne Waldman.

Baby's Pantoum

for Reed Bye

I lie in my crib midday this is
unusual I don't sleep really
Mamma's sweeping or else boiling water for tea
Other sounds are creak of chair & floor, water

dripping on heater from laundry, cat licking itself
Unusual I don't sleep really
unless it's dark night everyone in bed
Other sounds are creak of chair & floor, water

dripping on heater from laundry, cat licking itself
& occasional peck on typewriter, peck on my cheek
Unless it's dark night everyone in bed
I'm wide awake hungry wet lonely thinking

occasional peck on typewriter, peck on my cheek
My brain cells grow, I get bigger
I'm wide awake wet lonely hungry thinking
Then Mamma pulls out breast, says "Milky?"

My brain cells grow, I get bigger
This is my first Christmas in the world
Mamma pulls out breast, says "Milky?"
Daddy conducts a walking tour of house

This is my first Christmas in the world
I study knots in pine wood ceiling
Daddy conducts a walking tour of house
I study pictures of The Madonna del Parto, a

sweet-faced Buddha & Papago Indian girl
I study knots in pine wood ceiling
I like contrasts, stripes, eyes & hairlines
I study pictures of The Madonna del Parto, a

sweet-faced Buddha & Papago Indian girl
Life is colors, faces are moving
I like contrasts, stripes, eyes & hairlines
I don't know what I look like

Life is colors, faces are moving
They love me smiling
I don't know what I look like
I try to speak of baby joys & pains

They love me smiling
She takes me through a door, the wind howls
I try to speak of baby joys & pains
I'm squinting, light cuts through my skin

She takes me through a door, the wind howls
Furry shapes & large vehicles move close
I'm squinting, light cuts through my skin
World is vast I'm in it with closed eyes

I rest between her breasts, she places me on dry leaves
He carries me gently on his chest & shoulder
I'm locked in little dream, my fists are tight
They showed me moon in sky, was something

in my dream
He carries me gently on his chest & shoulder
He calls me sweet baby, good baby boy
They showed me moon in sky, was something

in my dream
She is moving quickly & dropping things
He calls me sweet baby, good baby boy
She sings hush go to sleep right now

She is moving quickly & dropping things
They rock my cradle, they hold me tightly in their arms
She sings hush go to sleep right now
She wears red nightgown, smells of spice & milk

They rock my cradle, they hold me tightly in their arms
I don't know any of these words or things yet
She wears a red nightgown, smells of spice & milk
He has something woolen & rough on

I don't know any of these words or things yet
I sit in my chair & watch what moves
He has something woolen & rough on
I can stretch & unfold as he holds me in the bath

I sit in my chair & watch what moves
I see when things are static or they dance
I can stretch & unfold as he holds me in the bath
Water is soft I came from water

I can see when things are static or they dance
like flames, the cat pouncing, shadows or light
streaming in
Water is soft I came from water

Not that long ago I was inside her
like flames, the cat pouncing, shadows or light
streaming in
I heard her voice then I remember now

 Not that long ago I was inside her
I lie in my crib midday this is
always changing, I am expanding toward you
Mamma's sweeping or else boiling water for tea.

Notice how the poet announces her deviation from a classic rendition by repeating lines two and four of the opening stanza in the exact same positions in stanza two. In stanza three, lines one and three are repetitions of stanza two's lines one and three rather than lines two and four. This spirit of play and invention continues throughout Waldman's poem. The repetitive lines circle us over and over again like the phenomenon of birth itself. The daily routine, even the monotony of child-rearing, becomes in Waldman's capable treatment a magical process. If ever a form existed that concentrates our attention on the moment, the pantoum is it. Weave it into your spiritual practice and see!

Here is a traditional example of a pantoum by Charles Baudelaire, translated from the French by Lord Alfred Douglas:

Harmonie du Soir

Now is the hour when, swinging in the breeze,
Each flower, like a censer, sheds its sweet.
The air is full of scents and melodies,
O languorous waltz! O swoon of dancing feet!

Each flower, like a censer, sheds its sweet,
The violins are like sad souls that cry,
O languorous waltz! O swoon of dancing feet!
A shrine of death and beauty is the sky.

The violins are like sad souls that cry,
Poor souls that hate the vast black night of Death;
A shrine of Death and Beauty is the sky.
Drowned in red blood, the Sun gives up his breath.

This soul that hates the vast black night of Death
Takes all the luminous past back tenderly.
Drowned in red blood, the Sun gives up his breath.
Thine image like a monstrance shines in me.

In Baudelaire's four quatrains, the second and fourth lines of one stanza become the first and third lines of the next.

And here is my own offering, inspired by my efforts in practice to generate compassion and relieve suffering for some national unsung heroes, high school teachers.

Pantoum of Acceptance

I'm teaching, for the eighteenth time in nine weeks,
the simple art of conjunctions when
to my question, "What is the difference between SUBordinate

And COordinate,"
the prettiest girl in the junior class says *Huh*?

The simple art of conjunctions: where
one part of equal or other value
(making the pretty girls from every class go *Huh*?)
joins with another, creating nuance.

One part of equal or other value
yearns for completion, a Venus moon, a wedding,
joining with another to create nuance,
layering simplicity with compound or complex ease.

"Yearn for completion, a Venus moon, a wedding,"
I tell them, "because apart your sentences will be incomplete."
Spurning simplicity and compound, complex ease,
The Chin looks up from his drool and mutters *So*?

I say again, "Apart, you will be incomplete,
a night-blind creature mumbling through broken teeth."
The Chin looks up from his drool and grumbles *So*?
This ain't no AP English class, you know?

A night-blind creature mumbling through broken teeth,
I glance at the clock, salvation in a bell.
I say, "This *isn't* AP English, I know."
The prettiest girl in the junior class goes *Huh*?

Exercise: Warming Up
Go back to the section on stanzas and write down one of the
examples. This is your beginning. Line two becomes line one

of your next stanza; line four becomes line three of this stanza, and so on. For example, this Keats quatrain:

Sweet, sweet is the greeting of eyes
And sweet is the voice in its greeting
When adieus have grown old and goodbyes
Fade away where old time is retreating

can proceed like this:

Sweet is the voice in its greeting
Yet bitter when promises made
Fade away where old time is retreating
And we run out of lemonade.

Let me be first to admit that this does not improve the original quatrain, but this can be a playful, excellent practice for contemplating the strands that bind us together through time. Try it, and think about all that you've learned so far from your writer-mentors, and from bringing poems into your spiritual practice.

Exercise: Listening for Pantoums
Pay special attention during a family meal to what is being said. Go to the table with the quiet goal of hearing and writing down four lines that stick with you like five-alarm chili. Later, write them down as a quatrain and compose a pantoum of at least four stanzas.

Exercise: Parrot Pantoums
If you do not actually know a parrot that speaks in pantoums, imagine teaching one to do so. Come up with phrases and

lines you think would sound memorable coming out of a beak. Share them with your friends, and perhaps with patrons at your local pet stores. There may even be a side career in this: teaching parrots poetry. Perhaps this is not as silly as it sounds. The sleeping potential audience for poetry is everywhere.

Exercise: Pantoum Headlines
On-line and print newspapers are excellent sources for pantoums. For example, here is a quatrain created from headlines of the paper on my desk:

> Illegals should come out from the shadows.
> Paragliders take a leap from Woodrat Mountain—
> A race of survival—Go with the flow.
> Find a good book for summer reading.

Headlines may or may not serve in your next stanza, or in the stanzas after that. I decided to use them.

> Paragliders take a leap from Woodrat Mountain.
> Her 'Bob' will be the one in the dress.
> Find a good book for summer reading—
> Road Runner gets a makeover.

So, scan the headlines and give it a try.

Exercise: Pantoum Journal
This exercise requires that you visit www.windchimewalker. net, where Patricia Lay-Dorsey decided to respond to the wars in Afghanistan and Iraq, and her long marriage, by keeping a journal in which each entry is a pantoum. Here is an example:

10/8/98

Our marriage is two spirals
Drawn by a single hand
Complete unto ourselves
Touching in the dance

Drawn by a single hand
Cosmos, Goddess, Fate
Touching in the dance
We mirror our best and our worst

Cosmos, Goddess, Fate
In motion unending
We mirror our best and our worst
Remaining lifetime partners

In motion unending
Complete unto ourselves
Remaining lifetime partners
Our marriage is two spirals

Think of a subject that would sustain you through many journal entries. It needs to be a subject that you deeply connect with, rather than a momentary focus or fascination. Once you have chosen a subject, write pantoum journal entries about it for at least a week. Share them with friends, or work with them in your daily spiritual practice.

15

Prose Poem:
Practice in Someone Else's Skin

The prose poem, especially for beginning readers and writers, can be the most confusing form in poetry. If we agree that prose is different from poetry, then how can we call a poem a *prose* poem? If the foundation of poetry is the line, not the prose sentence, why are prose poems written as if they were paragraphs in a novel or short story? As we try to answer these questions, it is wise to remember the adage that all is not as it seems. The fact of the prose poem does not upset our applecart. The prose poem is a playful, conscious act of subversion, a poetry form of dress-up. Consider how you change your spiritual practice to avoid getting stale. Writing a prose poem can be like that. Now to our questions.

The foundation of the prose poem remains the *line*, not the sentence. In a paragraph, our margins are justified, but in poetry every time we break a line we engage in an arbitrary act. The prose poem disguises this act but does not forsake the commitment to the line itself. In essence, we embed the line in the cloak of the sentence, relying on rhythm and imagery to suggest the hidden or submerged lines that emerge in our consciousness as we experience the poem. Consider the following:

Time

Willie was a good cop. Suspended, pending review, for shooting a fifteen-year-old in a lost neighborhood, he kept to himself at our church dinner munching my oatmeal cookies. It was awkward, but I sat beside him, waiting in case he needed to be touched. We exchanged nervous smiles and he stopped chewing. I could almost see the energy crackling all around him, and indeed we exchanged a little shock when I put my hand over his, but I kept it there. Together we were in a moment that didn't seem to be going anywhere and didn't need to. If either of us spoke it would change, so we didn't. But our minds did.

I don't know where Willie went, but I was traveling back through memory. I wanted to latch on to occasions when the moment was still. I thought of a newspaper headline: Martial Fervor Devastates Population, then a follow-up a few days later: Marshall Fervor Sues *Times*. Sometimes the saddest story makes me laugh, but only in a moment that's big enough to hold it. Air strikes expand a moment. Loved ones dying is a pretty good tonic for the racing clock hands. Of course, meditation contains one's thoughts in a context of expansive stillness, but even the smallest moment offers itself to awareness.

My daughter suffering the rejection of two playmates made me calm, and when the job I wanted eluded me, I entertained failure, then began to see doors and windows opening everywhere. Though the weight of the world rested on my shoulders, it was not heavy or more than I could bear. When the hummingbird came to the petunias I basked in its business, and though it zoomed away, our moment remained intact. So it was as we sat in our fold-out chairs in the gathering space, my hand covering Willie's. "Thank you," he said, bringing us back to our moment. We were no longer, as the man said, "shuddering at eternity, but eternity weeping and laughing over a moment."

The writing depends on concise imagery, tone, and pacing. The woman in the poem is doing her practice in real time, as she does all she can to be a spiritual friend to the tormented visitor. Despite appearances, the poem relies on the line rather than the sentence to zero in on their chance, momentary encounter, which changes both of them. This is a poem I recite and contemplate in practice when I'm meditating on compassion, forgiveness, justice, openness, and wholeness.

To the best of our knowledge, prose poetry originated in nineteenth-century France, where young poets embraced the form as a way of rebelling against the strict, standard six-stress line (the Alexandrine). By the end of the century, British Decadent poets, most notably Oscar Wilde, were attracted to the form and began writing in it. Many of the Decadent poets were homosexuals, so subjects and styles of their poems were discouraged by the older, mainstream literati. Two decades later, T. S. Eliot attacked the form on different grounds, though he did attempt to write a couple of prose poems. Robert Bly, a mentor for us all, has written with great brio in the form:

A Hollow Tree

I bend over an old hollow cottonwood stump, still standing, waist high, and look inside. Early spring. Its Siamese temple walls are all brown and ancient. The walls have been worked on by the intricate ones. Inside the hollow walls there is privacy and secrecy, dim light. And yet some creature has died here.

On the temple floor feathers, gray feathers, many of them with a fluted white tip. Many feathers. In the silence many feathers.

Here is another example by Raymond Carver:

Near Klamath

We stand around the burning oil drum
and we warm ourselves, our hands
and faces, in its pure lapping heat.
We raise steaming cups of coffee
to our lips and drink
with both hands. But we are salmon
fishermen and now we stamp our feet
on the snow and move upstream, slowly,
full of love, growing older with each step.

In an interview in *Another Chicago Magazine*, Peter Johnson said of the form: "Though I can't prove it, I think the prose poem wants to be funny. If Kierkegaard is right that 'the comical is present in every stage of life, for wherever there is life there is contradiction,' then what genre could be more contradictory than the prose poem, with its oxymoronic name and paradoxical nature? It steals the techniques of verse and discourses of prose, then shows up at the party flaunting them in the most unlikely ways."

Here is another example, again from Robert Bly:

Seeing Creeley for the First Time

Creeley sits on a chair, pulling up his knees to laugh, like a boy, looking very insecure, unsure, like a boy at school with pants too short. He looks astoundingly like a crow—it is unbelievable—even his hair is somehow "crow hair." Shining black, falling over his head that is full of determination to pester owls if he sees any. The beak is a crow beak, and the sideways look he gives, the head shoved slightly to the side by the bad eye, finishes it. And I suppose his language is crow language—no long open vowels, like the owl, no howls like the wolf, but instead short, faintly hollow, harsh sounds, that all together make something absolutely genuine, crow speech coming up from every feather, every source of that crow body and crow life.

The crows take very good care of their children, and are the most intelligent of birds, wary of human company, though when two or three fly over the countryside together, they look almost happy.

In practice, the prose poem requires that we pay special attention to breath and pacing. As you recite the lines of a prose poem in spiritual practice, notice how your breath and heartbeat speed up and slow down. Note how you aren't rushing to get through the words to the period; you're paying closer and closer attention to punctuation, to phrasing. In the process, perhaps you are making some subtle discoveries about your capacity for patience. You may also be unlocking some secrets about your own powers of articulation.

Exercise: Speed Kills, but Not Always

Open your notebooks or journals or laptops and speed-write without regard for line breaks. Do this for five to ten minutes. Keep the writing moving, and don't worry about making sense. Next, turn on the internal critic. Review what you have written. Try to punch up the dull spots with appropriate clusters of images. Share your results, and discuss what you've learned about the line and the sentence.

Here is part of an epistle (a letter to God or a congregation) by Mark Jarman. An epistle is a poem that often looks a lot like a prose poem.

In the Clouds

Simply by thinking I stood among the clouds. They surrounded and passed me, being and becoming. Blood released into clear water. Breath into cold air. Formlessness entering form, forced into form. Breathing felt huge then smaller than a cell. And I thought, "Don't the clouds themselves feel ambivalent between heaven and earth, hardly more substantial than their shadows? They come into being as randomly as we do. And they disintegrate. They go. What is the lifespan of a cloud? We want to float among them, loving the colossal, shot through with crooked pins of fire, towering side by side."

How did I get up there? I was thinking about changing my life and wanted to talk to a cloud, since clouds are always changing. And the clouds said, "How long has it been since you felt completely happy? Because you are always dissatisfied, always disappointed—it has been a long time. Talk to us. We are admired and disparaged. We are less than everything you compare us to except nothingness. We are not nothing. Talk to us. Our silence, like the new shapes we are forever assuming, will be sympathetic. In the clouds, you will understand yearning as you never have and come back to earth changed, who knows how?"

Exercise: Crack the Codes
Select three prose poems from books of poetry of your choosing. Write brief explications of each poem, paying special attention to how each poem works, how each one moves. Share your insights.

Exercise: Action Figures Included
Use the following and write a prose poem: the zoo, an office cubicle, a toy castle, blond hair, late spring, spring rolls, sweet and sour pork, birds like commas, stained curfews. You do not need to use these in the order in which they are listed here; you do not need to use every one of them. These are intended as catalysts. Use as many as you like and go for it.

Collaborative Exercise: Surrender to Rhythm and Process
Choose a partner. Begin what you hope will be a prose poem. When you get to the right-hand margin, stop and turn the

composition over to your partner. When she reaches the right-hand margin, you take over again. Continue this process until you decide that you've finished a poem. Try this at least three times. Don't worry about completing a thought, a line, or a sentence by the time you've reached the right-hand margin. Just keep going. Be agile, be quick, be inventive.

Four

Three Genres for Practice

16

Elegy:
Celebration and Letting Go

Mythologist, storyteller, and mentor to at-risk youths Michael J. Meade often makes the point that writers of tragedy are always trying to get at cathartic opportunities that create community. The events of September 11, 2001, presented such an opportunity on a worldwide scale. So does global warming; so did Hurricane Katrina, and the devastating Southern California fires of 2007. But in addition to these global and national catharses, every single death presents an opportunity for people to come together, as every death sets the stage for a birth or rebirth, a new life.

Elegies, poems written in praise of the dead, are especially powerful in spiritual practice because they commemorate these cathartic opportunities by stirring up, then calming, our deepest pools of grief. In the process, we the still-living are reborn. We band together to pass through the trial of an important death, and we are changed. Elegies infuse this process with a palpable energy and, later on, remind us of where we were and how far we've come.

Elegies can really be about anything we care deeply about and lose: people we love, animals, a sacred place, a job, or team. The form provides closure. It's a way of saying goodbye while celebrating who or what is gone.

In some sense, an elegy is also about the writer. It is an emotional acknowledgment on his or her part that all things are impermanent, which is itself a profound spiritual understanding.

The following poem was written by an anonymous soldier in Northern Ireland who foresaw his impending death.

Do Not Stand at My Grave and Weep

Do not stand at my grave and weep;
I am not there. I do not sleep.
I am a thousand winds that blow.
I am the diamond glints on snow.
I am the sunlight on ripened grain.
I am the gentle autumn rain.
When you awaken in the morning's hush
I am the swift uplifting rush
Of quiet birds in circled flight.
I am the soft stars that shine at night.
Do not stand at my grave and cry;
I am not there; I did not die.

Like many elegies, the poem transforms a natural lament over death into a birth, a celebration of immortality. In fact, mutability, the inevitability and power of change, is at the heart of a form that so deeply meditates on death. *Everything dies*, the poet begins, *and I am staggeringly saddened by it. I miss my departed loved ones so much I don't know how I can go on. So I sing to death, to the departed who are still somehow a part of me. In my song, if I am lucky, death blossoms, becoming another necessary, beautiful part of the experience of life itself. I celebrate the departed. I honor the times we had. I celebrate, and I pass it on, preserving history and helping those who come after me to better understand the rituals that define and deepen human existence.* And *that* is poetry as spiritual practice.

Here is Robinson Jeffers's elegy for Haig, a beloved pet.

The House Dog's Grave

I've changed my ways a little; I cannot now
Run with you in the evenings along the shore,
Except in a kind of dream; and you, if you dream a moment,
You see me there.

So leave awhile the paw-marks on the front door
Where I used to scratch to go out or in,
And you'd soon open; leave on the kitchen floor
The marks of my drinking-pan.

I cannot lie by your fire as I used to do
On the warm stone,
Nor at the foot of your bed; no, all the nights through
I lie alone.

But your kind thought has laid me less than six feet
Outside your window where firelight so often plays,
And where you sit to read—and I fear often grieving for me—
Every night your lamplight lies on my place.

You, man and woman, live so long, it is hard
To think of you ever dying.
A little dog would get tired, living so long.
I hope that when you are lying

Under the ground like me your lives will appear
As good and joyful as mine.
No, dears, that's too much hope: you are not so well cared for
As I have been.

And never have known the passionate undivided
Fidelities that I knew.
Your minds are perhaps too active, too many-sided . . .
But to me you were true.

You were never masters, but friends. I was your friend.
I loved you well, and was loved. Deep love endures
To the end and far past the end. If this is my end,
I am not lonely. I am not afraid. I am still yours.

   (Haig, an English bulldog)

Elegy is all about closing the gap between the visible and
the invisible worlds. Declarations of immortality alone are
not enough. Our anonymous Irish poet compares himself to
wind, snow, rain, grain, a morning's sound, birds in flight, and
stars. These are appropriate. We respond to each one emotion-
ally, recognizing in them our own humble identification with
the natural world and the mysterious powers that organize it.
In an elegy we are intent on honoring someone dear to us, and
we also aim to prepare for our own deaths, and for what comes
after. The best elegies are heartbreaking and reassuring. They

make us feel like weeping, and they make us feel like offering up a cheer.

In 1980, six weeks after my mother's midsummer death, a vivid dream of my sister closest in age to me woke me up in the middle of the night. As far as I knew, my sister had not visited a dream of mine in years. I thought it odd but eventually drifted back to sleep. In the morning, my sister-in-law called to tell me that Beverly had committed suicide. About the time that I was waking from a dream, my sister half a continent away was taping the windows and doors shut in her garage while her four young children slept in the attached house. Then she climbed into her car and started the motor. She was not discovered until morning. She was thirty-six.

Nineteen eighty brought a summer of death to our family. In retrospect, it also brought us a lifetime of debate and evaluation. We found out soon enough what drove my sister to take her life, then we wondered how she could do such a thing with her own children sleeping nearby. In time, we all faced the challenge of reconciliation and forgiveness.

As a writer, I expected to meet the challenge through verse, but nothing came. For years, nothing came. Just when I thought I'd arrived at a place where I could forgive her, I would think of one or more of her children, of the difficulties they faced in their later lives, and I would be seized by anger. What right did she have, despite her woe, to wound her children? But then, what right did I have to judge her? Didn't my faith teach me that my only responsibility was to love her? More than twenty years later, while doing my daily writing in my journal, I surprised myself by writing a poem to my sister at last. It occurred to me that her children would live to be older than she had ever been, that despite everything their lives had gone on. Before I fully understood the significance of what I was doing, I was writing a sonnet, but also an elegy of love and forgiveness.

Elegy in August

Sleep, little sister, far from pain.
Water smooths out stones in the river
As memory calms the chaos
You left behind. Rest easy, sister,
Your babies are older than you ever were.
Even the stain will fade
When none are left to remember
The calls for help you never made.

After burning, blackberry bushes
Struggle up through ash, and love, resilient,
Blooms in all seasons, even for you
Who suffered and could not tell what was right
As you hurled yourself, suddenly
Spiraling upward to darkness or light.

Elegy helps us examine our lives and make sense of loss. It shows us how to sing about life and how to pray for everyone in it.

Dylan Thomas's *Do Not Go Gentle into That Good Night* is a great villanelle and elegy all in one. In the poem, as Thomas exhorts his dying father to die bravely, without surrender, Thomas is also urging himself on.

Elegies are also a way of saying thank you, of celebrating a life lived well. In February 2004, the poet and founding editor of the *Hudson Review*, Frederick Morgan, died in New

York at eighty. In his exemplary life, Fred not only wrote some beautiful, memorable poems, he discovered, developed, and sustained the work, and in many cases the personal lives, of at least three generations of poets and writers, including William Carlos Williams, Ezra Pound, Wallace Stevens, Anne Sexton, Maxine Kumin, W. S. Merwin, Louis Simpson, Anthony Hecht, Emily Grosholz, Mark Jarman, Dana Gioia, and David Mason, among many, many others. To dozens of poets and writers of my generation, Fred was a valuable and generous mentor, but he was an even greater spiritual adviser and friend. Shortly after his death, Mark Jarman composed this poignant tribute:

Frederick Morgan

How do we send our friend into the night?
Having seen so many different kinds of death,
suicidal, accidental, the blow of illness,
still he remains associated with life.

How do we send him out, away from life?
Sporting his beret, swinging his cane,
or reclining, talking easily with us,
surrounding him, his bed like a little boat.

He has seen so many different kinds of death.
He has faced the emptiness so many times
and turned back to look at us with a smile
of benevolence, which was no mask.

The world with his friends in it was like a picture
he stood before, marveling and appraising,
loving the odd art each of us offered
under his frank, forgiving lamplight.

Still to take pleasure is the best thing
after it too is revealed to be the mind's play
as, if you live long enough, all things
will be revealed. How shall we send him out?

After a lunch with us, before a walk,
having tasted the cold salads and sparkling wine
and his laugh, that combination of delights,
not strictly of Apollo or Dionysus.

Let it be, as he has said, a good day
as cloud shadows zebra-stripe the walls
of sun-bright skyscrapers, and all appears
to step with us as we walk with him a ways—

the skyscrapers, the zebras and the clouds,
and the good day striding out of sight.

Throughout its many graceful movements, this poem acknowledges the departed's greater age and wisdom. The echo of the first line in line five, the question *How do we send him out?*—brings home to us the inevitability of casting out the dead. I do not mean *casting out* as in discarding them. I am thinking here of the responsibility that friends and lovers bear in attending one who is about to die. In Jarman's elegy, the language is all about movement and travel. The passage of time, the walking, the clouds, and of course "his bed like a little boat" evoke the fleeting nature of life and our need to observe and participate in all transformations. In fact, we live for this, a "combination of delight" that should be life itself. The living send the dead out and hope for the day when, "if you live long enough, all things/will be revealed."

Exercise: Goodbyes That Never End
Try to write elegies of any length and form for a relative, a close family friend, and a pet. Remember that an emotional distance of sorts makes for the most deeply felt emotional connection. Ample comparisons cast as metaphors and similes cannot hurt.

Exercise: You Can Go Back
Think about a home place you loved but lost. Write an elegy for it.

Exercise: Sensitive Poetry Pack Rat
We acquire and lose things with staggering rapidity. Compose an elegy in tercets for a beloved item that has largely lost its importance or significance for you.

Exercise: Body Parts
It never hurts to think outlandishly when experimenting with poetry. For example, the sixteenth-century astronomer Tycho Brahe was missing most of his nose and wore a specially crafted beak of silver for public occasions. Imagine what it would be like if you were missing your nose, or your mouth, or ears. Compose an elegy in couplets about the missing part.

Exercise: The Story Muscle
The poem by Dana Gioia that follows is a narrative (it tells a story about planting a magical tree) and an elegy for a lost son.

Planting a Sequoia

All afternoon my brothers and I have worked in the orchard,
Digging this hole, laying you into it, carefully packing the soil.
Rain blackened the horizon, but cold winds kept it over the
    Pacific,
And the sky above us stayed the dull gray
Of an old year coming to an end.

In Sicily a father plants a tree to celebrate his first son's birth—
An olive or a fig tree—a sign that the earth has one more life
    to bear.
I would have done the same, proudly laying new stock into my
    Father's orchard,
A green sapling rising among the twisted apple boughs,
A promise of new fruit in other autumns.

But today we kneel in the cold planting you, our native giant,
Defying the practical custom of our fathers,
Wrapping in your roots a lock of hair, a piece of an infant's
    birth cord,
All that remains above earth of a first-born son,
A few stray atoms brought back to the elements.

We will give you what we can—our labor and our soil,
Water drawn from the earth when the skies fail,
Nights scented with the ocean fog, days softened by the
    circuit of bees.
We plant you in the corner of the grove, bathed in western
    light,
A slender shoot against the sunset.

And when our family is no more, all of his unborn brothers
    Dead,
Every niece and nephew scattered, the house torn down,
His mother's beauty ashes in the air,
I want you to stand among strangers, all young and
    ephemeral to you,
Silently keeping the secret of your birth.

Create an elegy that also tells a story. Perhaps you can write about something that you lost, something that was very important to you. Provide narrative details about how the thing was lost, and how the loss was discovered.

Collaborative Exercise: Group Grief

Work with any number of friends to write an elegy about the environment, which concerns all of us. Try another about education, the tax code, a religious event. Alternate on composition of lines. Mentor one another as you strive to create a memorable poem.

Finally, work at least two of your favorite elegies into your own daily spiritual practice. Over a month, note in your journal how these poems alter your practice, and you.

17

Free Verse:
Diligent Individuality

The Sky and the Earth

Here we are, but why? What are we here for?
As this question rests in my head, the world keeps turning,
and everything passes me by. Friends I thought were so
    important disappear
All but one
Things I thought I couldn't live without fade away
All but one
Feelings I thought I could never feel erupt inside me,
And the answer appears in my head,
As obvious as a mountain on the horizon,
Love,
But not fleeting love.
It's the love that makes people sing,
The love that shakes people to their knees.
Nothing compares to the beautiful love shared
between the sky and the earth,
For the lord resides in the sky, and his creations reside on the
    earth.

    (Eoghan McDowell)

The greatest influences on the creation of American free verse were the King James Bible and the French Symbolist poets.

Walt Whitman, our poetry father and primary mentor, was our first great free-verse poet. His poems do not adhere to a strict metrical pattern. Rather, they immerse readers in powerful rhythmic cadences that often echo the Bible and feature memorable imagery, explosive, syntactical surprises, parallelism, and irregular rhyme. Many poets before him, including notables such as John Milton and Matthew Arnold, experimented with free verse of this kind, but it was Whitman who produced an undeniable body of influential work in this vein.

Rebelling against their own status quo, the French Symbolists of the late nineteenth century (Arthur Rimbaud foremost among them) focused on syntax and grammar rather than counting syllables (metrics) in poems. They described their practice as vers libre, from which our own free verse takes its name. T. S. Eliot, who was devoted to French poetry (and composed some poems in French), became an early-twentieth-century American-British advocate of vers libre, and the cause was soon expanded by Amy Lowell, Ezra Pound, and other poets. Their poems succeeded in challenging what was perceived then as the formal stodginess that had worn out mainstream poetry. By the 1960s, free verse had become the dominant method in American poetry, but by the 1980s, American poetry experienced a revival of traditional form, which in turn rejuvenated free-verse poems that had become predictable and stodgy in their own right. Schools of poetry, like patterns of history, go round and round.

Here is a poem by Ezra Pound—a poet who wrote formal and free-verse poems—that makes peace with the once-puzzling influence of Walt Whitman.

A Pact

I make a pact with you, Walt Whitman—
I have detested you long enough.
I come to you as a grown child
Who has had a pig-headed father;
I am old enough now to make friends.
It was you that broke the new wood,
Now is the time for carving.
We have one sap and one root—
Let there be commerce between us.

The line governs this poem, but it is not a line determined by metrical units. Pound creates an edgy, conversational tone, a one-sided dialogue if you will. Though all the lines but one are end-stopped, the poem's movement is a headlong rush to the closing declaration—*Let there be commerce between us.* This is the triumph of a harnessed cadence, a consistent, controlled rhythm.

This poem is also an excellent example of a speaker putting himself in the role of apprentice and addressing a mentor. Pound reminds us that mentors, at certain times, can be very annoying. But not all the time. Spiritual practice teaches us that many obstacles and irritations we see around us really exist inside us. They're our obstacles, and we must clear them to progress. At some point, if we are lucky, we accept the mentor's valuable lesson, his gift.

Another Pound poem of just two lines famously makes a case for vers libre.

In a Station of the Metro

The apparition of these faces in the crowd;
Petals on a wet, black bough.

Free verse must pack memorable imagery, creating an itch in the brain that won't be satisfied by absentminded scratching. It must also contain a cadenced rhythm that is convincing in its integrity and urgency. Relaxing an emphasis on meter and rhyme requires compensations if the writing is to become something other than rambling prose, if in fact it is to become a poem.

Successful free-verse poems are created by a poet's argument with existing forms. That is why such poems contain hauntings of traditional forms. Free-verse poems splinter or fracture inherited forms, then put the pieces together again in different shapes and patterns that fit a distinctive rhythm.

Finally, I hope we can agree that free-verse poems are as applicable in spiritual practice as traditionally patterned, formal poems. Free verse, after all, is poetry. If a free-verse poem is created from an intention to benefit others, to generate truth, beauty, forgiveness, peace, and compassion, then it is still the language of devotion. It's true that free-verse poems are generally harder to remember than formal poems, but they're not impossible to lodge in the heart and brain. Perhaps you might think of them as more relaxed conversations with the Divine, the Beloved, or God.

Here is an example of a free-verse poem-prayer by Nancy Willard. Notice the way she repeats the word at the end of the first three clauses. This device is called epiphora.

The Speckled Hen's Morning Song to Biddy Early

Let the speckled hen praise her.
Let the nine nations of slugs honor her.
Let the ten tribes of sparrows rejoice in her:

High-stepper, moon-catcher,
keeper of starlight in dark jars,
protector of pigs, saver of spiders.

Praise her from whom all cracked corn flows,
for whom the stars go willingly to roost,
for whom the gold loaf in the sky rises.

Try including free-verse poems like these in your own practice and see what transformations take place!

Exercise: Imagery and Cadence

Make a list of ten images. Consult an excerpt from Walt Whitman's *Leaves of Grass*. Try to write a poem using your ten images and Whitman's cadence as you hear it. Discuss the results with your friends.

Exercise: Fracture Prose

Select a long paragraph from any novel. Fracture the paragraph and its sentences, creating lines of poetry from the fragments. Delete and add what you deem necessary. Share your results with friends, and discuss the differences between the line and the sentence.

Collaborative Exercise: Meter and Rhyme to Rhythm

For this exercise, work with two of your friends. Select a poem written in a traditional form. Dissect it, dispensing with the rhyme and meter. Using what is left, turn the words into a free-verse poem. What is gained, and what is lost, in the process? Share your revelations, and write them down in your journal.

You can also reverse and turn a free-verse poem into a formal poem. In fact, many formal poems are developed in this way.

18

Story Poems:
Practicing Deep Delight

The great California poet Robinson Jeffers wrote, "To feel greatly, and understand greatly, and express greatly the natural beauty is the sole business of poetry." I find much of his poetry exhilarating and devotional.

For much of his life, Jeffers had a contentious relationship with God, and for Jeffers God *was* the natural world. Jeffers distrusted modern civilization's orthodox interpretation of a supreme being, its God figures in whose names countless millions were butchered in a century of war. His pantheistic beliefs would not have seemed alien to ancient Celts and other cultures that nurtured a close relationship to the earth. Witness these lines from his poem *Natural Music.*

> The old voice of the ocean, the bird-chatter of little rivers,
> (Winter has given them gold for silver
> To stain their water and bladed green for brown to line their
> banks)
> From different throats into one language.
> So I believe if we were strong enough to listen without

Divisions of desire and terror
To the storm of the sick nations, the rage of the hunger-
    smitten cities,
Those voices also would be found
Clean as a child's; or like some girl's breathing who dances
    alone
By the ocean-shore, dreaming of lovers.

Every human being *feels*, whether one wants to or not. Our life experience fills us with joy and, at times, heartbreaking sorrow. Much of our time seems to be filled with unexceptional moments. The more we have, the less satisfied we feel, the more bored we become. We harbor personal guilt, shame, and loneliness, and when these feelings get the better of us, we blame others for them. *My good friend is not friend enough. My boyfriend isn't willing to change his behavior to make me happy. My teacher is unfair, doesn't really like me, and that's why I am not doing well in his class. The editor who rejected my poems is an idiot. My parents don't understand me. My apartment is a dump; I'll always live in dumps. I hate my hair, my gut, my clunky shoes. My dog is annoying. I practice and practice, but don't notice any progress!*

This litany of complaints probably sounds familiar, doesn't it? These are just some of the words of the self-destructive games we play, the things we tell ourselves to shut us off from others and keep ourselves down. These are the poisons that threaten to destroy the natural beauty every moment of every day.

We use them because we're afraid. We're afraid that we really are as inept, unattractive, and useless as some in our lives always told us we were. We're afraid that if we allow other people to get too close, they'll just end up hurting us when we least expect it. We build our bunkers, we grow our thick shells, and we hunker down inside them. When loneliness becomes too powerful, we conjure another victim's lament to comfort us, to justify our retreat from life.

But all life is joy and change and surprise. To feel greatly and understand greatly the natural beauty is to be open to life, to all that it offers. Gu Fangwen, a practitioner of Chinese medicine, says that "in old China, Chinese doctors claimed to have 'secret knowledge' of herbs and ancient family remedies. For me the secret knowledge is knowledge of the patient and his relationship with you and others."

This is the secret of poetry, too, especially narrative poetry. To express greatly the natural beauty is to become a poet in all that we say and do, a builder who contributes to and nurtures an ever-expanding community in work, in family, and love. Poets who tell stories take up this responsibility with unbound happiness. In this excerpt from *Song of the Open Road*, part of his epic *Leaves of Grass*, Walt Whitman expressed it thus:

4

The earth expanding right hand and left hand,
The picture alive, every part in its best light,
The music falling in where it is wanted, and stopping where
       it is not wanted,
The cheerful voice of the public road, the gay fresh senti-
       ment of the road.

O highway I travel, do you say to me *Do not leave me*?
Do you say *Venture not—if you leave me you are lost*?

Do you say *I am already prepared, I am well-beaten and
      undenied, adhere to me?*

O public road, I say back I am not afraid to leave you, yet I
      love you,
You express me better than I can express myself,
You shall be more to me than my poem.

I think heroic deeds were all conceiv'd in the open air, and
      all free poems also,
I think I could stop here myself and do miracles,
I think whatever I shall meet on the road I shall like, and
      whoever beholds me shall like me,
I think whoever I see must be happy.

Poetry, like all art, periodically reinvents itself through renovation of language and subject. In the late eighteenth and early nineteenth centuries, William Wordsworth wrote poems in everyday language about the farmers, women, tinkers, and traveling people of his home, Northumbria in England. To a classicist of the period, Wordsworth's poems were shocking, even distasteful, yet eventually they became one of the great standards against which future poetry would be measured. In *My Heart Leaps Up*, Wordsworth honors a deep, almost innocent relationship to creation and the natural world, and celebrates childhood in the process:

My heart leaps up when I behold
A rainbow in the sky:
So was it when my life began;
So is it now I am a man;

So be it when I shall grow old,
Or let me die!
The Child is father of the Man;
And I could wish my days to be
Bound each to each by natural piety.

Wordsworth's younger contemporary, George Gordon, Lord Byron, wrote exuberant, rollicking, and exotic epics that became wildly popular and made their author one of the first media celebrities around the world. Byron's long stories in verse were brilliant, entertaining precursors of our episodic television comedies and dramas. Here is the opening stanza from *The Prisoner of Chillon*, a verse tale of religious persecution and perseverance.

My hair is gray, but not with years,
    Nor grew it white
    In a single night,
As men's have grown from sudden fears;
My limbs are bow'd, though not with toil,
But rusted with a vile repose,
For they have been a dungeon's spoil,
And mine has been the fate of those
To whom the goodly earth and air
Are bann'd, and barr'd—forbidden fare;
But this was for my father's faith
I suffer'd chains and courted death;
That father perish'd at the stake
For tenets he would not forsake;
And for the same his lineal race,
In darkness found a dwelling-place.

We were seven—who now are one,
    Six in youth, and one in age,
Finish'd as they had begun,
    Proud of Persecution's rage;
One in fire, and two in field
Their belief with blood have seal'd,
Dying as their father died,
For the God their foes denied;
Three were in a dungeon cast,
Of whom this wreck is left the last.

In fact, every generation produces poets who develop into important verse storytellers. In the twentieth century in America, Robinson Jeffers was one. He lived in Carmel at Big Sur in a house and tower he built himself from wood and granite, and wrote several long poems that are as rich and dramatic as the best novels and films. One, *The Women at Point Sur*, tells the story of a charismatic figure most of us would readily recognize from having seen evangelical preachers on television.

Edwin Arlington Robinson and Robert Frost wrote narrative poems of various lengths about salesmen and farmers, drunks and merchants, couples and backwoods crazy folk. Robert Penn Warren wrote a wonderful narrative poem about the artist and chronicler of birds, John James Audubon, and Robert Service is still celebrated for his spirited ballads of the West.

Narrative's traditional form in poetry, the ballad, probably predates writing itself. These early folk verses were meant to be sung, and were often composed by illiterate or semiliterate peasants and traveling people. Story-songs were passed on orally from generation to generation, some eventually vanishing altogether or morphing into different versions to suit a different time and its people. In *The English and Scottish Popular Ballads* (1882–1898), Francis J. Child collected 305 authentic folk ballads. What follows is an example, a traditional Scottish ballad by an anonymous author. In the 1960s, Bob Dylan recorded a version of it.

Bonny Barbara Allan

It was in and about the Martinmas time,
    When the green leaves were afalling,
That Sir John Graeme, in the West Country,
    Fell in love with Barbara Allan.

He sent his men down through the town,
    To the place where she was dwelling;
"O haste and come to my master dear,
    Gin ye be Barbara Allan."

O hooly, hooly rose she up,
    To the place where he was lying,
And when she drew the curtain by:
    "Young man, I think you're dying."

"O it's I'm sick, and very, very sick,
    And 'tis a' for Barbara Allan."—
"O the better for me ye's ever be,
    Though your heart's blood were aspilling.

"O dinna ye mind, young man," said she,
    "When ye was in the tavern adrinking,

That ye made the health gae round and round,
　　And slighted Barbara Allan?"

He turned his face unto the wall,
　　And death was with him dealing:
"Adieu, adieu my dear friends all,
　　And be kind to Barbara Allan."

And slowly, slowly raise she up,
　　And slowly, slowly left him,
And sighing said she could not stay,
　　Since death of life had reft him.

She had not gane a mile but twa
　　When she heard the dead-bell ringing,
And every jow that the dead-bell geid,
　　It cried, "Woe to Barbara Allan!"

"O mother, mother, make my bed!
　　O make it saft and narrow!
Since my love died for me today,
　　I'll die for him tomorrow."

The poem, in quatrains of four stress/three stress, four stress/three stress meter (the common ballad measure), features irregular rhyme and what amounts to a refrain with the repetition of Barbara Allan's name. The poem also includes some Scottish dialect, which makes sense if you read the lines aloud. In stanza two, line four, *gin* means "if"; in stanza three, line one, *hooly* means "quickly," or "swiftly"; in stanza five, line one, *dinna* means "never," and *gae* in line three means "go"; in stanza eight, line one, *gane* and *twa* mean "gone" and "two"; in line three, *jow* and *geid* mean "stroke" and "gave"; in stanza nine, line two, *saft* means "soft."

The poem tells a story about a dying man who calls his true love to his bedside. She goes reluctantly, slowly, and once there she is cold, unforgiving. She chastises the invalid for a recent transgression, real or imagined, in the tavern. Thus reproached, the man turns his face to the wall, says goodbye to his friends, and begs them to be kind to the woman who cannot be kind to him. Rather than wait with him for his death to come calling, she leaves with nothing stronger than a sigh. In the final stanza, Barbara Allan takes to her bed, suggesting that she suffers regret, even guilt, and will die for her dead love tomorrow.

Some readers see in this a belated softening in Barbara Allan, but doesn't it sound like a popular refrain? Many people put off confronting difficult or powerful emotions, often tragically missing opportunities to connect with people they love. Another famous character, Scarlett O'Hara in *Gone with the Wind*, would say, when life becomes too emotional, too tough, "I'll think about it tomorrow!"

Narrative poems tell the stories of diverse people and make use of all of poetry's parts—plot, description, meditation, dialogue, character, lyricism, argumentation—to create a complete tale that delivers a reading experience not unlike that of a good novel or short story. A major difference is that a poem of this kind will do in thirty pages what a novel would do in three hundred. Compression is critical to the success of a narrative poem. It will make the skin of your skull constrict and tingle. Like any good poem, it will contain the potential of memorable song because it enters you as the language of devotion. Casey Bailey has pointed out on his Word.com blog that "the peculiar excellence of scripture is that it communicates truth about God poetically largely through narrative."

More than poets and literary scholars have discovered the restorative power of storytelling in verse. Rita Charon, for instance, is an internist with a Ph.D. in literature and director of the groundbreaking Program in Narrative Medicine at Columbia University. Like the Chinese doctor we met a moment ago, she and an increasing number of colleagues nationwide believe in what she calls "narrative competence." Their belief is that narratology should be studied in the same way, and with the same seriousness, that students study anatomy. Listening well and responding to a patient's "illness narrative" will be as important to recovery as physical therapy. Verse storytelling spiritually centers the patient, improves communication, promotes health, and empowers communities.

Here is a narrative poem I use in a long practice during which I contemplate injustice, sacrifice, tolerance, and forgiveness. The poem tells the family story of a Japanese immigrant to the United States and his family through much of the twentieth century.

All I Took with the Sun

Takeo's Voyage, 1929

Because I would not come into the farm
My jewel, Japan, my perfect wife and dreams
Diminished as our ship flew out of sight
Down tunnels leading to America.
I thought *I'll make my fortune, then return.*
I told my troubles to the stars above
And wrote in a ledger, a present from my teacher.

I played cards with a little group of men,
Some of whom believed they'd never see
The shores of home again. Disputing that,
I said that any one of us could be
A man of means, if not of property.

The sea nights conjured never-ending dreams
As I paced wordlessly among the shades,
A Shadow-Boy with no brave song. I mourned
My future, my green past. The shadows spoke
In riddles, softly, whether to conceal
Their meaning, or to vex me, I couldn't tell.
It's bad to be so much inside one's head.

I see now, many years from there, how like
A dish of rain I was, so small and pure
And ignorant, a moony wanderer.
How like the fish the seabirds gobbled up!
So Fate had marked my brother for the land,
And me for this adventure. That's what it was.
No lofty seeking, but sheer adventuring.
Is that a word? I'm seven decades in
America, and still I panic when
My grammar is uncertain. I met so many
Yanks who made me feel inferior.

Seattle, 1929

A beefy, red-cheeked man the size of two
Of us came down to the dock to pick out workers,
But most of what he said eluded us.

It was disgraceful the way he jabbed at us,
But we were tired, grateful to be getting
Off the boat, and so we followed him
To town, to a sprawling boardinghouse and bowls
Of tacky rice, our first meal in the States.
That night some of us slept on pallets hinged
To rough-hewn walls, while others slept on floors.

Sleeping so, it's easy to rise early.
Another big American was there
To show us work, and by the noon sit-down
We Japanese were Yankee railroad men!
We worked long shifts and volunteered for more
Because the work made tolerable our fear,
The fear that comes of being far from home,
The fear that comes when you're invited to
A party and you show up looking like
The foreigner you are. We worked like that,
Finding in misery a common cause.

Hiroko's Passage, 1936

My mother died,
My father, too,
Before I spoke
Or walked the room
Or fought my way
To where I'd be
Across the sea.

On board, my bed
Was by the cook's,
A four-foot plank
That folded out
And dangled from chains.
I'd hug the wall,
Afraid I'd fall.

I knew that I
Had traveled far
From orphanage
To dock, to star,
From empty space
And setting sun
To this new one.

Takeo's Vision, 1936

I met her ship. She fell out in a state
Of mourning for the home she'd left behind.
On land again she wobbled for a day.
We spoke in nervous bursts. I couldn't look
At her, while she walked staring at the ground,
Her possessions in a sack I transferred from
Her back to mine; a courtesy, a way
Of showing her that I was glad she'd come,
That life in our new country would be fine.

That night as she slept deeply in our bed
I'd set up by the fire, I felt the presence
Of generations past, as if her dream

Had called them to join us in that tiny room.
By firelight I wandered over her,
But only with my eyes. I marveled at
Her hands and feet, so delicate and small,
Her oval face the color of cherry wood.

I must have slept, for when I woke,
All stiff and cold, Hiroko poured a bowl
Of tea and served it with an almost-smile.
We murmured to each other in morning voices
Thick and halting, the rain a fragrant wash
Outside the open window. We huddled close.
She brushed a cobweb from her hair, and with
That sweeping motion of her hand, so like
A swallow making elegant the air
Inside a barn, my heart filled up with her.

My focus and intentions were so clear
I couldn't wait to leave the railroad life
And lease the farm. I had one all picked out,
A thirty-acre parcel owned by a man
My foreman sent me to. Within a week
My dear and I were married and moved in.

Hiroko's Vision, 1937

The passage hard, I'd had my storm-tossed dreams
About the kind of man collecting me.
He met me at the ship, a falcon-man—
Tight in his body, full of courtesy.
We bowed, and as we walked I studied him

Without him knowing it. His skin shone bronze
In pools of light we entered, left behind.
A time or two I caught a shadow-smile,
And in his features I could see his aunt,
Who with his grandfather arranged this plan.
I saw his posture, straight and fine, a wing
In sunlight knifing above the earth. I saw
That we'd work well together. Our family
Would be the beds we'd make up anywhere.
Watching my partner sleeping by the fire,
I saw that his bones, his flesh, his soul were good.
I allowed it into my heart—our silent pact.

The Years

The whistles shouting *work, release, step down*
Were all I knew until my bride-to-be
Arrived. Hiroko cleaned and took in laundry
Seven days a week, but we found time
For picnics at the lake, and Sunday romps
Among the islands of Puget Sound. It's said
The world we toil in of necessity
Is narrow, but the one that opens up
To us through love unfolds like fields of lilies
Rolling on as far as the eye can see.

Soon we became the farmers we were born
To be. Five miles from Santa Rita we
Got down to work on twenty acres of
The richest bottomland I'd seen since home.
We'd beat the sun to work and trail it back,

And as our crop of corn and beans came in,
We almost forgot: We could not own the land,
Being alien. Oh, there was plenty
Reminding us that we were foreign, strange,
A threat to security, the economy.
We'd feel it in an awkward turning away
While offering to ease a neighbor's task,
Or in a glance we were not meant to see
On trips to town, or on eviction days.
Three times in seven years, our landowners
Informed us they were sorry, we had to go.

So, by lamplight, in late hours, I studied hard
To be a citizen, and in the spring
Of 1941 I took the oath
That made me, with my labor, *American*,
Able to own land. And soon we did.
Down south, near Watsonville, I coveted
A fifty-acre farm. The ground was right
For garlic, artichoke, and brussel sprout.
That magic earth, it seemed, could almost grow
A crop without our help. Hiroko said
Our land was giving birth to better days,
And she was right—for almost one sweet year.

Then, early in 1943, a man
Came out to see us from the government.
He did not look us in the eye, but read
From documents he pulled out of his hat.
I didn't follow all he had to say
Because my ears were playing tricks on me.
Like Cyprus branches, they filled with Pacific fog.

Driving out, his tires kicked up a rock
That nicked my cheek. I wiped the blood away,
And watched his lights grow small. Late that night
Hiroko said, "I'm done with crying now."
She said to me, "You are a citizen."

How did I miss the State's decision? How
Did I resist resisting it? Not one
Of us could fight, for doing so would be
Like a confession, treason in time of war.
The relocation planners might have prayed
For us to rise against them with rakes and shovels.
How easy then to massacre us all.
I wanted to understand. I wanted them
To understand, and then apologize.

On a balmy day an army truck arrived
To take us to the train. Hiroko held
Our baby. We carried clothes sacks on our backs,
And on a whim I ran into the house
To grab the sewing machine, thinking we
Could make new clothes as long as we were gone.

Hiroko and the Camps, 1944

We did not think, as soldiers drove us off,
That we would never see our farm again.
We rode so long my body became numb
From heat and dust, the shaking of the truck.
Not much was said until we reached the train,
When panic ripped our voices saying *Where?*

Where are we going? Terror seized us then.
The boxcars were thick with heat and sweat.
Some women said *Take Heart* and tried to sing,
But soon their voices cracked, their songs sighed out
In misery. In Pinedale we got out
To barbed wire, dust, and barking uniforms
That pressed us into registration lines.
We paced the hardpan yard and settled in barracks,
Some bitter, others optimistic that
We'd soon be going home. For many, the day-
to-day deranged us, even as we set
Up schools and services, elected some
To settle disputes and govern our routines.
We focused on our gardens, sewing, games,
But everyone was drawn to walk the fence
Where dogs would snarl and lunge if you got close.
In winter we were never warm enough;
In summer it was always sweltering.

One positive—we made community
With strangers we would not have known outside.
We women cooked and sewed and cleaned the place
That through our labor imitated home.
Some men would stand around, not knowing what
To put their bodies to. The dust was awful.
It swarmed us, swirling through the barracks boards.
We never got the grime out of our clothes.
One day became another. Nothing new.
Hiss of boiling water, clumps of rice
In earthen bowls, the drinking water warm.
Sunlight thudded against the barracks walls
Where men, deflated, slouched and shielded their eyes.

Our son turned two on our next moving day.
The bus driver, over his shoulder, said
That he was taking us to Tule Lake.
A few broke down. The rest of us maintained
Our dignity, or so we told ourselves.
Some said we'd like it better by a lake,
And maybe we would be allowed to swim.
That cheered us up until we reached the camp,
Which looked just like the one we'd left behind.
The air like death, the stubble lakebed cracked.

We moved to our third camp in '45,
A higher place, Heart Mountain, Wyoming,
Where Gene was born. The thin air disagreed
With all of us. Both boys were suffering
Most of the time, and many elders died
In the six months we wasted there. At last,
The day of our emancipation came.
We were too stunned, too weak to celebrate
As we made fast our packing, stood in line
For checking out, and wondered where we'd go.
Our homes were gone, so there was nothing to
Return to or revive. Our keepers signed
And stamped our exit papers, and sent us back
Into the world without apology.

Takeo, 1976

Hiroko was our rock and waterfall
In the concentration camps. She focused us
On little things—the daily tending of

A garden plot, methodical raking of
Our compound dirt, the relocation groups
In which we shared the songs and poetry
We could recall. So we were ready for
The future when it came, like any day.
The trouble was, the future wasn't sure
What it would do with us. A man we knew,
Abducted from Alhambra, said it would
Be smart to settle up in Oregon.
We took his word for it, I signed a lease
To work a hundred acres east of Salem.
In seven years I bought the property,
Expanded, built a house, acquired two trucks.

So it was more than thirty years before
My family could buy the farm I'll soon
Be buried on. My darling wife has gone
Ahead, and I've the urge to follow her,
To take my place beside her in the plot
Beyond the barn. My sons have married well,
Two small-boned girls from home who love, like us,
The work and seasons of the land. They have
Strong sons, who have it in them to grow the farm
Beyond my grandest dreams. I am content.

Now that I'm old, my redneck neighbors come
To ask advice about rotation crops,
How they might grow still sweeter onions,
Which markets they should pay attention to.
Enjoying their respect, I tell what I know,
But I keep to myself the knowledge that I am

The hawk that circles their fields, the mystery bird
They admire and fear. I am the dinner guest
They never really know. My family
Is made of this, though I believe it's true
That each new generation distances
Itself a little more from its received
Intolerance, and one day our own blood
Will blossom in a marriage with a race
That scorned and hounded us. The wind chill drops.
After I walk the fields, it's time I slept.

Exercise: Become Someone You're Not
Adopt the persona of someone else, anyone, even someone in
your own family. Write a narrative poem of at least two pages
in the first person. Experience in your dramatic monologue
the freedom of being, for a time, another person.

Exercise: Your Own Epiphany
Examine your own life, and choose its most dramatic incident.
Create a narrator who is not you, and set that individual the
task of telling the story of that identity-defining incident.

Exercise: The Woman, or the Man (or Both), in You
Tell a story in verse from the point of view of someone of the
opposite sex.

Collaborative Exercise: Pair Up, Witness, Listen
Writing stories in verse depends a great deal on listening. One
must first become a reliable, compassionate witness before
one is able to discover and tell a densely compressed story in
a poem.

Pair up with a friend and go together to visit an owner of a business (a bookstore, ice-cream shop, bakery, laundry, car dealership, for example), or a farmer or rancher, a government official, gardener, day-care worker, or someone in the medical profession. Don't simply interview that person, but really listen to what he or she has to say. Experience your visit at his pace. Learn all you can. Later, compare notes. Then see if together, or separately, you are able to bear witness in a poem that illuminates the life you have been privileged to learn about.

Keep in mind that you are not simply reporting, which is a valuable kind of writing called journalism, but delving beneath and beyond the facts in your poem. Frequently, the key to a character's personality and story can be revealed through a certain expression, habit, or personal tic. For example, poker players are always observing fellow players for their individual *tell*, the giveaway, the sign that a player is bluffing or has a really good hand. It may be that the player nervously drums his fingers on the table when he has really good cards, or he doesn't look any of the other players in the eye when he's bluffing. His tell gives him away.

Just about everybody owns a series of tells that are the keys to their stories. In a narrative poem, it's the poet's task to recognize and unveil them. Then see how it works for you to invite these people and stories into your daily practice.

In Closing

We are seekers of faith, each and every one of us, and all that we discover, all that we learn, is integrated into our spiritual growth. Eventually, if we are wholly present and engaged, we pass on much of what we learned, much of what we've become, to apprentices who see us as mentors.

Poetry enriches and deepens spiritual practice, inspires practice-specific mentor-apprentice relationships, and immeasurably contributes to creating mentor-apprentice relationships in all walks of life. Today, poetry is more important than ever in creating and maintaining a life of compassion and awareness. The poet and scholar James Finn Cotter gets right to this point in his book *A New Life: Learning the Way of Omega*, which reflects on the importance of poetry. "Human beings," Cotter writes, "have never been in more need of the myths of poetry. Especially in our contemporary culture, we . . . have to hear poems said by heart again in woods and squares and over the kitchen table. Poetry must become part of everyday conversation."

Cotter is calling for the reunion of poetry and spirituality, a state the ancient world knew well. Separating poetry from spiritual practice weakens both. Don't we have enough history behind us to know that much? Don't we hunger to bring the essence of our spiritual practice into everyday conversation, into our daily lives?

The Poem

It discovers by night
what the day hid from it.
Sometimes it turns itself
into an animal.
In summer it takes long walks
by itself where meadows
fold back from ditches.
Once it stood still
in a quiet row of machines.
Who knows
what it is thinking?
   (Donald Hall)

Poetry's power is spiritual, mysterious, and wide-ranging. As a little girl, the Arizona writer and teacher Meg Files was misdiagnosed with leukemia. She was hospitalized and not expected to live. In her hospital bed she wrote her first poems. When her diagnosis was corrected, when she recovered and was allowed to go home, she understood something important, something she would never forget.

"I'd written poems and I hadn't died," she said. "Therefore, poetry saved my life. . . . For me, writing and mortality are forever bound."

Poetry is the utterance that the better angels of our natures long to hear.

As we come to the end of our shared spiritual journey, keep in mind that your practice is ongoing as long as you live and write. In her song *Words*, Lucinda Williams (the daughter, incidentally, of the wonderful American poet Miller Williams) offers her own powerful tribute to writing: *You can't kill my words, they know no bounds/My words are strong and they don't make me sick/They still remain my only companion/Loyal and true to the very end/They'll never ever completely abandon/Ever give up the paper and the pen.*

I hope you feel good about yourself at this point. You should celebrate and delight in the effort you've put into your practice through your poems and reading, for you have come far. Now, in closing, let's turn to the spiritual mother of American poetry, Emily Dickinson. After our time together, we can all appreciate the sentiment she so gracefully expresses.

I reckon—when I count at all—
First—Poets—Then the Sun—
Then Summer—Then the Heaven of God—
And then—the List is done—

But, looking back—the First so seems
To Comprehend the Whole—
The Others look a needless Show—
So I write—Poets—All—

Their Summer—lasts a Solid Year—
They can afford a Sun
The East—would deem extravagant—
And if the Further Heaven—

Be Beautiful as they prepare
For Those who worship Them—
It is too difficult a Grace—
To justify the Dream—

Poems Included as Illustrations Within Chapters

The Shape of Practice: Waking Up Through Poetry

Words, Metaphor, Simile

Alliteration and Assonance

Sonnet: Be Nimble, Be Quick

Villanelle: The Power of Echo

Sestina: Repetition in Practice

Limerick and Epigram: Playful and Laughing

Ghazal: Attention and Wonder

Pantoum: Questing, Devotion, Gratitude

Prose Poem: Practice in Someone Else's Skin

Elegy: Celebration and Letting Go

Acknowledgments

I feel boundless gratitude for many who made it possible for me to write and publish *Poetry as Spiritual Practice.* My agent Linda Roghaar believed in me and made a miracle with the swiftness of barn swallows. My editor Leslie Meredith and her assistant Donna Loffredo guided and encouraged me, making the book so much better than it ever was in my hands alone. Edith Lewis and her copyediting staff, and copy editor Fred Wiemer, corrected gaffes and omissions that would have marred the book. Shaman Jane Galer pushed me and my manuscript out the door into the wide world. Lama Bruce Newman, Father Jeremy Driscoll, and Father Pat Walsh have been able readers of a friend's heart. April Elliott Kent's enthusiasm and inspiring Web design have made so many workdays sparkle. The hymn writer and therapist Maureen Hicks may be the most meticulous, generous, and skillful listener I've ever known. Randy and Carole McDowell, Barbara and Howard Campbell, and my children—Dylan, Eoghan, Branden, and Jane—are family rocks and safe harbors. Randy Gilbert and Peggy McColl are treasured mentors in marketing and life. Finally, I'm grateful for my fellow travelers of our four-year Marig Munsel class in Tibetan Buddhism at Tashi Choling on Mount Ashland.

Permissions

These poems, in part or in whole, appear here with the following generous permission:

"Paper Cranes" by Thomas Merton, *The Collected Poems of Thomas Merton*. New York: New Directions Press, 1977, appears with permission of the publisher.

"Bud & Night Terrors" by Cyrus Watson; "Fishing" by Gretchen Fletcher; and "The Management of Poems" by Dori Appel appear with permission of the authors.

"A Calling" by Maxine Kumin, *Selected Poems 1960–1990*. New York: W. W. Norton & Company (new ed. 1998), appears with permission of the publisher.

"Talking with the Dead" by Robert McDowell was originally published in *Sewanee Review* and appears with the author's permission.

"Records" by George Hitchcock, *One-Man Boat: The George Hitchcock Reader*. Ashland, OR: Story Line Press, 2003, appears with permission of the publisher.

"What the Cleaning Lady Knows" by Ginger Andrews, *An Honest Answer*. Ashland, OR: Story Line Press, 2001, appears with permission of the publisher.

Excerpt from "Deciding the Course My Education Should Take" by Clemens Starck, *Journeyman's Wages*. Ashland, OR: Story Line Press, 1998, appears with permission of the publisher.

"House Through Leaves" by Elise Paschen, *Infidelities*. Ashland, OR: Story Line Press, 1996, appears with permission of the publisher.

"Optimist" and "Ellenalliv for Lew" by R. S. Gwynn, *No Word of Farewell: New and Selected Poems*. Ashland, OR: Story Line Press, 2001, appears with permission of the publisher.

"Villanelle for Our Time" by F. R. Scott, reprinted with permission of William Toye, literary executor for the estate of F. R. Scott.

"Epidemic: 1918" by Robert McDowell, reprinted with the author's permission.

"Love Letters" by Diane Thiel, *Echolocations*. Ashland, OR: Story Line Press, 2000, reprinted with permission of the publisher.

"Bordello" by Lewis Turco, *The Collected Lyrics of Lewis Turco/Wesli Court*. Scottsdale, AZ: StarCloudPress, 2004, reprinted with the author's permission.

"Sestina #4" by James Cummins, *The Whole Truth*. Pittsburgh, PA: Carnegie-Mellon University Press, 2003, reprinted with the author's permission.

"3 Epigrams by Martial," translated by J. V. Cunningham, *The Collected Poems and Epigrams of J. V. Cunningham*. Athens, OH: Ohio University Press/Swallow Press, www.ohioswallow.com, 1971, reprinted with permission of the publisher.

"Pale hands I loved beside the Shalimar" by Agha Shahid Ali, *A Nostalgist's Map of America*. New York: W. W. Norton and Company, 1991, reprinted with permission of the publisher.

"Sam's Ghazal" by Elise Paschen, *Infidelities*. Ashland, OR: Story Line Press, 1997, reprinted with permission of the publisher.

"Parent's Pantoum" by Carolyn Kizer, *A Formal Feeling Comes: Poems in Form by Contemporary Women*, ed. by Annie Finch. Ashland, OR: Story Line Press, 1994, reprinted with permission of the publisher.

"Baby's Pantoum" by Anne Waldman, *A Formal Feeling Comes: Poems in Form by Contemporary Women*, ed. by Annie Finch. Ashland, OR: Story Line Press, 1994, reprinted with permission of the author.

"Pantoum of Acceptance" by Robert McDowell, reprinted with permission of the author.

"10/8/98" by Patricia Lay-Dorsey, www.windchimewalker.com, reprinted with permission of the author.

"Time" by Robert McDowell, reprinted with permission of the author.

"A Hollow Tree" and "Seeing Creeley for the First Time" by Robert Bly, *The Morning Glory*. San Francisco: Kayak Press, 3rd printing, 1969, reprinted with permission of the publisher.

"Near Klamath" by Raymond Carver, *Winter Insomnia*. San Francisco: Kayak Press, 1970, reprinted with permission of the author.

"In the Clouds" by Mark Jarman, *Epistles*. Nashville: Sarabande Press, 2007, reprinted with permission of the publisher.

"The House Dog's Grave" by Robinson Jeffers, *Selected Poems of Robinson Jeffers*. New York: Random House, 1975, reprinted with permission of the publisher.

"Elegy in August" by Robert McDowell. Originally appeared in *Poetry*, reprinted with permission of the author.

"Frederick Morgan" by Mark Jarman, reprinted with permission of the author.

"Planting a Sequoia" by Dana Gioia, *Planting a Sequoia Poems*. West Chester: Aralia Press, 1991, reprinted with permission of the publisher.

"The Sky and the Earth" by Eoghan McDowell, reprinted with permission of the author.

"The Speckled Hen's Morning Song to Biddy Early" by Nancy Willard, reprinted from *A Formal Feeling Comes: Poems in Form By Contemporary Women*, ed. by Annie Finch. Ashland, OR: Story Line Press, 1994, reprinted with permission of the author.

"Natural Music" by Robinson Jeffers, *Selected Poems of Robinson Jeffers*, ed. by Tim Hunt. Palo Alto, CA: Stanford University Press, reprinted with permission of the publisher.

"All I Took with the Sun" by Robert McDowell, originally appeared in *The Hudson Review*. It is reprinted here with the author's permission.

"The Poem" by Donald Hall, *Old & New Poems*. Boston: Mariner Books/Houghton Mifflin Company, 1990, reprinted with permission of the publisher.

About the Author

ROBERT MCDOWELL is the author of three books of poetry, coauthor of two volumes of literary theory, cotranslator of a collection of stories, and the editor of three anthologies. His poems, stories, essays, and reviews have appeared in hundreds of anthologies and periodicals here and abroad, including *Best American Poetry*, *Poetry*, the *New Criterion*, *Sewanee Review*, and the *Hudson Review*. He has taught in the graduate seminars at Bennington College, the University of Southern Indiana, UC Santa Cruz, and at the Taos Summer Writers' Conference, Sewanee Writers' Conference, Mendocino Coast Writers Conference, Killybegs Festival, West Chester Conference on Form and Narrative, and many other venues.

McDowell also worked as founding publisher-editor of Story Line Press, where he selected and edited 250 books and created *The Poetry Hour*, a program for radio. He has lived on and worked a seed-grass farm, run sheep, raised horses, served as a fundraiser for AmericorpVISTA, and taught high school English, journalism, and drama. McDowell offers one-on-one mentoring, and coaching for businesses and groups interested in improving spiritual awareness, listening, communication, writing, and presentation skills. His Web site is www.robertmcdowell.net.